Folens
Essential
Non-fiction

Models for Writing

Peter Ellison

© 2002 Folens Limited, on behalf of the author.

United Kingdom: Folens Publishers, Apex Business Centre, Boscombe Road, Dunstable, LU5 4RL.
Email: folens@folens.com

Ireland: Folens Publishers, Greenhills Road, Tallaght, Dublin 24.
Email: info@folens.ie

Poland: JUKA, ul. Renesansowa 38, Warsaw 01-905.

Editor: Nancy Terry
Layout artist: 2i Design, Cambridge
Cover design: 2i Design, Cambridge

First published 2002 by Folens Limited.

British Library Cataloguing in Publication Data. A catalogue record for this publication is available from the British Library.

ISBN 184303–2317

Acknowledgements

Text extracts: *Seize the Moment* by Helen Sharman, published by Victor Gollancz, a division of the Orion Publishing Group; Extract from *My Left Foot* by Christy Brown published by Secker & Warburg. Used by permission of the Random House Group Limited; *The good ship 'Tree'* by Darren Shan from the *Times Educational Supplement* © Darren Shan, 2001; *Jewell New Obituary* from *The Daily Telegraph*, 4 July 1998 © Telegraph Group Limited (1998); *Shakespeare, William* from World Book Online – Americas Edition. URL: http://www.worldbookonline.com/wbol/wbpage/na/ar/co/504520 © World Book Inc., 2002. By permission of the publisher; *Success Stuns Harry Potter Author* by Audrey Wood from the Associated Press; *Lemony Snicket's Deliciously Sour Tales* by Julia Durango. Reprinted with permission from *The Daily Times*, Ottawa, Illinois, USA and Julia Durango © copyright 2000; *Shrek* reviewed by Ferret, IOFilm, URL: http://www.insideout.co.uk/films/s/shrek.shtml. Reproduced with permission of IOFilm; *Animal Magic* by Charles Spencer from *The Daily Telegraph*, 21 October 1999 © Telegraph Group Limited (1999); *The Complete and Utter Idiot's Guide to Making a Baloney Sandwich* by David Neilsen from The Brunching Shuttlecocks website, URL: http://www.brunching.com/features/idiotsandwich.html. Reproduced with permission of David Neilsen, Brunching Shuttlecocks; *Las Vegas* by Bill Bryson: Copyright © 1989 from *The Lost Continent* by Bill Bryson, published by Black Swan, an imprint of Transworld Publishers Ltd. Reproduced by permission of Greene and Heaton Ltd; *Announcing the BOOK* from the IFLA website. We invite the copyright holder of this extract to contact the publishers; *Shampoo* by Dustin Perkins from McSweeney's Magazine website, URL: http://www.mcsweeneys.net/2000/11/15shampoo.html. Reproduced by permission of the author, Dustin Perkins; 'Advice, like youth, is probably wasted on the young' ('Everybody's free') by Mary Schmich from *The Chicago Tribune*, 7 June 1997; *Those who can, teach* from the TTA website; *Diary of a home-educator* (Anon) from *The Sunday Times*. This article first appeared in *The Sunday Times*, 4 March 2001; *Does learning at home work?* by Diana Appleyard from *The Daily Telegraph*, 21 October 1997 © Telegraph Group Limited (1997); *Helping children learn* from Parentlineplus; *Smart shirt rolls up its own sleeeves* by Robert Uhlig from *The Daily Telegraph*, 28 November 2001 © Telegraph Group Limited (2001); *How time travel will work* from How Stuff Works Express website, URL: http://www.howstuffworks.com/ hsww-timetravel.htm; *More Letters to Uncle Albert* by Russell Stannard, published by Faber and Faber; *Elephants and humans* by Craig Kasnoff, Bagheera.com, URL: http://www.bagheera.com/ inthewild/van_animal_elephant.htm; *Copper – Living proof that hunt saboteurs save lives* by Andy from the Hunt Saboteurs website, URL: http://has.enviroweb.org/features/copper.html. Reproduced with permission of the Hunt Saboteurs Association; *The hunter's view: A job has been done for the farmer* from *The Guardian* 11 October 1999 © The Guardian; *Accidents should happen* by Frank Furedi, from *The Daily Telegraph* 30 March 2001 © Telegraph Group Limited (2001); *International Walk to School Day* by iwalktoschool.org. Reproduced with permission of Robert Smith of iwalktoschool.org; *The woman who hangs today* from *The Daily Mirror*, 13 July 1955 © Mirror Syndication International

Photographs: Cover image: Corbis Stock Market; p9 My life, your life: Novosti/Topham; p10 Space shuttle: Corbis Stock Market; p12 Girl in space: John Lamb/Tony Stone; p28 Harry Potter: supplied by Capital Pictures; p31 Review and rewind: Corbis Stock Market; p36 *Shrek*: supplied by Capital Pictures; p38 *Lion King* © Disney. Photo by Catherine Ashmore; p41 Inside laughter: Clive McDonnell/Ace photo agency; p46 Las Vegas: Corbis Stock Market; p55 Sunbather: © Popperfoto/Bob Thomas ; p57 Teach you a lesson: Corbis Stock Market; p58 Those who can teach: DigitalVision; p63 Young boy: Popperfoto; p71 Let me explain: Eric Meola/The Image Bank; p83 Hear my voice: Corbis Stock Market; p90 bike: Corbis Stock Market; p96 Ruth Ellis: Popperfoto

Contents

Introduction

Essential Non-fiction

Your questions answered:

What's in this book?

The best thing to do is to flick through it and see what catches your eye: after all, there are 28 texts to choose from, each chosen carefully. However – in one simple explanation – you will find a wide variety of basic to more challenging non-fiction texts designed to make you laugh, think about issues and learn about new areas.

So what's so essential about it?

The texts have been carefully chosen to present some of the best examples of non-fiction writing around – and to show you how professional writers do it. Using this book might make your own writing stronger.

Why does it have that other title, 'Models for Writing'?

Well, although you will read each text first, the point of the book is to help you learn about the techniques good writers use in order to get their message across, or entertain the reader. In other words, it will refer you to the key features of texts and provide you with models from which you can learn.

How do I know what these key features are?

The book is divided into seven sections. The way that the texts are grouped will help you make comparisons and contrasts between them, and to see how writers deal with the same issue in different ways.

Also, every text is preceded by a section called 'About the text'. This asks you to look out for key things, at Word, Sentence and Text level, as you read. In this way, the key features will be clear to you.

In addition, the very first section, 'Take the text tour', takes you on a quick trip around some of the main non-fiction types, to ensure you know the basics before you begin.

Sounds good, but why should I take this seriously?

The writer is Peter Ellison, a Literacy Adviser and experienced English teacher, examiner and writer. He is very well placed to give you advice, and to provide you with interesting and wide-ranging examples of non-fiction texts he has selected.

Ultimately, you should read the texts to enjoy them, but through reading and studying them, you will improve your writing skills. This will be of benefit to all your school work, and will prepare you for examinations and other forms of assessment. Most of all, the book will make you more like a real writer, in the real world.

Take the text tour

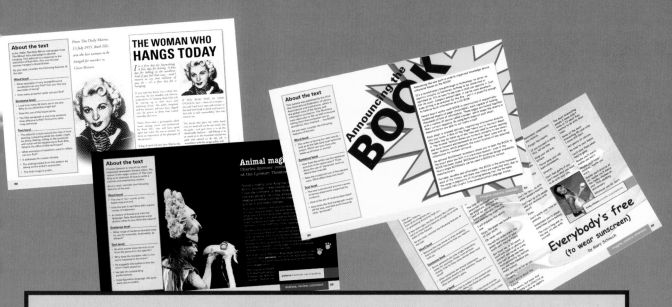

About the chapter

Before you read through the main chapters, take this quick tour to see the different text types you will meet:

- information
- instructions
- recount
- persuasion
- explanation
- discursive writing.

Each type of text is written for a different purpose. As you read each extract, consider the features that characterise its text type. For example, instructions contain a great number of imperative verbs such as *make* and *put*.

conventions of non-fiction

Information

Purpose: To describe things as they are as precisely as possible. It usually answers the question, 'What?'

Word level

- Technical terms are explained in the text (see *incisors* in the extract).
- Simple but precise language.

Sentence level

- Uses brackets and commas to fit in as much information as possible.
- Written in the present tense.

Text level

- Talks about elephants in general, rather than about a particular elephant.
- The text is designed to tell the reader as much as possible about elephants in as short a space as possible.
- This type of text will normally be split up into chapters, each one dealing with a different aspect of the subject. What might the other chapters of this particular text be about?
- You can find a longer extract from this text on page 80.

Recount

Purpose: To retell events.

Word level

- Uses lots of connectives of time (see *then* and *now* in the extract) so that the reader understands the order of events.
- Focuses on an individual or group so it is often written in the first person (see *I* and *we* in the extract).

Sentence level

- Written in the past tense.
- Uses a variety of sentence structures to retain the reader's interest.

Text level

- Written in chronological order – that is, as things happen.
- Contains quite a lot of detail to keep it lively.
- Encourages the reader to imagine him or herself in the place of the writer.
- You can find a longer extract from this text on page 11.

The elephant

At first glance, African and Asian elephants appear the same. An informed eye, however, can distinguish between the two species. An African bull elephant (adult male) can weigh as much as 14 000 to 16 000 pounds (6 300 to 7 300kg) and grow to 13 feet (4 metres) at the shoulder. Its smaller relative, the Asian elephant, averages 5 000 pounds (2 300kg) and 9 to 10 feet (3 metres) tall. The African elephant is sway-backed and has a tapering head, while the Asian elephant is hump-backed and has a huge, domed head. Probably the most interesting difference between the two species is their ears. Oddly, the African elephant's large ears match the shape of the African continent, and the Asian elephant's smaller ears match the shape of India.

Elongated incisors (front teeth), more commonly known as tusks, grow up to 7 inches (18cm) per year. All elephants have tusks, except for female Asian elephants. The largest of the African bulls' tusks can weigh as much as 160 pounds (73kg) and grow to 12 feet (4 metres) long. Most animals this big, however, are gone; they were the first to be killed for their ivory.

Seize the Moment

In my earphones, a voice from the bunker said, "Five minutes to go. Please close the masks of your helmets."

The three of us obeyed, then confirmed. Our call-sign was ozone, and we identified ourselves by crew number. I was the last to confirm, and so I said, "Ozone 3, ozone 3, my helmet is shut. We are in the preparation regime, ready to go."

The bunker replied, "Understood, ozone 3. We are also in that regime. Everything on board is correct and we are now ready to launch."

A little later, the voice said, "Two minutes." Then it said, "One minute."

Now that we were not moving around or reaching for the controls above us, it was comfortable to be sitting there in the spacesuit.

Explanation

Purpose: To explain how something works or the reasons why something has happened. It usually answers the question, 'Why?' or 'How?'

Word level

- Uses causal connectives (see *so* and *but* in the extract).

Sentence level

- Written in the present tense.

- Often uses lots of short paragraphs.

Text level

- The text often starts simply but gradually becomes more complex.

- Usually written in a series of short steps.

- Often leads to a conclusion.

- You can find a longer extract from this text on page 74.

Instructions

Purpose: To tell the reader what to do by taking them through a sequence of steps. Usually answers the question, 'How do I ... ?' or 'What do I do if ... ?'

Word level

- Uses imperative verbs (see *start*, *take* and *use* in the extract).

- Employs connectives of time (see *now* and *after* in the extract) so that the reader can follow the sequence.

Sentence level

- Often uses numbered or bullet-pointed sentences.

- Generally uses short sentences.

Text level

- Often uses diagrams to help the reader to follow.

- Needs to be very clear and precise.

- Often includes quantities or sizes (see *2 or 3 tablespoons* in the extract).

How time travel will work

The key to speeding up time travel and allowing us to jump into the future is to build vehicles that can travel at the speed of light – or at least near light speed. Light speed equals 186 000 miles per second! That is about 11 million times faster than a car travelling at 60mph! Scientists claim that time actually slows down for you as you near light speed. So, if you had a time machine that allowed you to travel at the speed of light, time would slow down for you – but it would remain the same for those not in the time machine.

But here's the hitch. Scientists don't believe that matter can actually reach the speed of light. The good news is that we don't need to travel at the speed of light to travel through time. In fact, we already have spaceships that can jump into the future.

Making your own fake shrunken head

Start with an apple. The larger the better. It will shrink quite a bit. Then remove most of the peel using a vegetable peeler. You can leave a little at the top and bottom. Now take a small knife and carve a face. It will take some practice getting it right, but after several attempts you should get a feel for it. Here are some tips:

- Make the features (nose, mouth) big. Shrinkage will reduce them more than you will realise.

- Use toothpicks for the details.

- Round and smooth the surface of the 'head' using a rag or paper towel.

- Try not to gouge too deeply with the knife as cuts left in the surface may be magnified after shrinking.

Once carved, you must 'pickle' your apple/head. Immerse it in a solution of 1/2 cup of salt mixed with about 4–6 cups of water. Adding 2 or 3 tablespoons of lemon juice will keep it from oxidising. Let it soak for 24 hours. Remove it from the water. Straighten out a paperclip or stiff wire and form a small loop in one end. This will be used to pass a string through. Stick the clip through the top of the apple and down through the bottom. Bend the clip at the bottom to hold it in place. The apple/head is then hung from a string by the clip. You will need to hang it where it will stay dry. After about 2 or 3 weeks, it should be ready.

Persuasion

Purpose: To persuade the reader to do something or to argue a case or point of view.

Word level

- Often uses powerful words (see *cruel and terrifying death* in the extract).

Sentence level

- Sentences are linked to make a logical case (see *Copper's case explodes the myth that ...* and *His general condition is proof that ...* in the extract).

- Written in the present tense although examples may be given in the past.

Text level

- Does not include an opposing point of view except to disprove it.

- Makes a strong argument.

- Often starts with a statement of belief.

- Often repeats words or phrases for effect.

- Sometimes uses poetic techniques like metaphors or similes.

- You will find a longer version of the text on page 84.

Discursive writing

Purpose: To present arguments from differing viewpoints.

Word level

- Uses logical connectives (see *but*, *because* and *while* in the extract).

Sentence level

- Often uses complex sentences so that the writer can convey complex ideas.

Text level

- Gives equal weight to two or more opposing viewpoints.

- Often includes questions to be explored by the writer.

- May not come up with an answer.

- Has to guide the reader carefully through complex arguments.

- Uses evidence to back up opinions.

- Often quotes from other sources, for instance, experts.

- May include the writer's own views but does not have to.

- You will find a longer version of the text on page 62.

Copper, the fox

After medical treatment, Copper spent some weeks recovering and recuperating in a wildlife hospital. He was released, fit and well, into a non-hunting area in March 1999.

Copper's case explodes the myth that a hunted fox is either killed 'by a quick nip to the back of the neck' or gets away. The bite marks to Copper's hind legs – and Andy's eye-witness account – show that hounds will snap at any part of a hunted fox to bring it down.

His general condition is proof that, as in the case of hunted stags (highlighted in the 1997 Bateson Report), hunted foxes suffer intolerable levels of stress as a direct result of the chase itself. The hunting fraternity have always known this. In 1960, Lord Paget wrote: "Pain and suffering is inflicted on animals in the name of sport. Nobody who has seen a beaten fox dragging his stiff limbs into the ditch in which he knows he will soon die, can doubt this proposition."

That's why, although Copper's rescue was successful, Andy doesn't consider February 6th a good day's sabbing. "For us a good day is one where the hunt don't get to chase an animal at all," he explains. Covering scent with a mixture of water and citronella oil, or using horn calls to draw the hounds away from a hunted animal are both tactics used by saboteurs to stop a chase before it even begins! Until hunting is banned, the only chance animals like Copper have to evade a cruel and terrifying death, is people like Andy ...

Does learning at home work?

In America, there are now over a million home-schoolers and several hundred dedicated websites. Britain is slowly following suit.

The big question is whether home education – increasingly made more feasible by computer technology – is a sensible option for so many more children. Are parents being swept along by this trend, scared off by all the horror stories around state education?

... Meighan argues that home-educated children – because of the fact that they follow their own interests – are 'turned on' independent learners, while so many school-educated children are 'turned off' dependent learners. But because of the very fact that these children are allowed to follow their own interests most of the time, the question remains as to how they will cope with the world once they move out of their comfortable, private learning environment and whether they will ever really fit in.

2

My life, your life

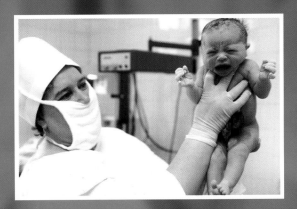

About the chapter

How do writers describe the interesting and important experiences in their lives?
How do they write perceptively about someone else's life?

In this section, you will read a variety of extracts from autobiographies and
biographical writing.

inform, explain, describe

About the text

The extract you are about to read is taken from the autobiography of Helen Sharman, who was the first British woman to take part in a space expedition.

As you read, consider the following features of the text:

Word level

- How does the writer mix together technical language and everyday language?

Sentence level

- What impact does her variety of sentences create? For example, how does she use short sentences to create tension?

- Where does she link paragraphs together by using connectives (especially of time)?

- What different tenses does she use for effect (such as moving from past to present)?

Text level

- How does she encourage the reader to identify with her experience by including everyday physical description? (For example, her mention of her cold feet.)

- How does she use changes of pace and language style at key moments in the text?

Seize the Moment

by Helen Sharman

In my earphones, a voice from the bunker said, "Five minutes to go. Please close the masks of your helmets."

The three of us obeyed, then confirmed. Our call-sign was *ozone*, and we identified ourselves by crew number. I was the last to confirm, and so I said, "Ozone 3, ozone 3, my helmet is shut. We are in the preparation regime, ready to go."

The bunker replied, "Understood, ozone 3. We are also in that regime. Everything on board is correct and we are now ready to launch."

A little later, the voice said, "Two minutes." Then it said, "One minute."

Now that we were not moving around or reaching for the controls above us, it was comfortable to be sitting there in the spacesuit. I glanced at the little **talisman**, swinging from the hatch above us. I felt the pressure of Tolya's elbow against mine. I could hear the quiet hiss of static in the speaker against my ear. Sergei said nothing, Tolya said nothing; the voice from the bunker was silent. It was a moment of stillness, of final waiting. My feet were still cold.

> **talisman** a good luck charm

Far away, deep below, there came a rumbling noise as the rocket engines ignited. On the control panel the on-board clock had started automatically; we were nominally one second into the mission, then two, and the engines still rumbled far below. Three seconds and the rumbling grew louder and, as the four launch-gantries swung away, I could feel vibration but no sense of acceleration. I knew we must have left the ground and were in that momentary limbo where the rocket seems to balance precariously on its thrust, surely destined to topple. But the engines continued to roar beneath us and the instruments confirmed that we were away from the tower, that acceleration was beginning to build, and we could feel the pressure of g-forces growing steadily against us.

When I next looked at the clock we were twenty seconds into the flight – and above us the talisman was taut on its string, no longer as free to swing. I could now sense the rocket's power, not only from the vibrations coming through the seat but also from the increasing press of acceleration. The clock showed that forty seconds had elapsed. The voice from the bunker confirmed the successful launch and Sergei briefly responded. G-forces continued to grow; the rocket was getting lighter as the fuel burned away and we were picking up speed.

After 115 seconds came the first of several loud bumps and bangs: the escape rocket on the nose of the craft was being jettisoned. At this point we were 46 kilometres from the ground on the threshold of space. Three seconds later there was another jolt, this one bigger and from below, as the first-stage booster rockets separated from us. This was the moment we passed the 50 kilometres mark, the height the Russians usually designate as the beginning of space.

Our smooth acceleration continued as the rocket grew lighter; now we were using the second-stage engine. This was the centrally mounted main engine, used from the moment of lift-off. It was still burning steadily when,

165 seconds into the flight, the protective fairing that covered the windows was jettisoned, no longer needed to protect the spacecraft from the atmosphere as there was little atmosphere left outside!

Sunlight streamed in. I looked down at the Earth. We were already over the Pacific!

Tolya said, "What can you see? What can you see?" He had no window, and was dazzled by the golden sunlight pouring in.

I could see the curvature of the Earth! Speckly white clouds! A brilliant azure sea! The blackness of space! Now I knew I was where the theory told me I should be – out from the world, above the blue skies and diamond-studded clouds. Dreams sometimes do come true and I felt so alive!

The craft was rotating and the view turned away from me. Then it was Sergei's turn to see. Poor Tolya could only glimpse it.

Sergei said, "It's snowing up here! The ice is

breaking off!"

In the sunlight, in the vacuum outside my window, I too could see that chunks of ice were breaking away from the body of the rocket. If we had been in the atmosphere they would have been whipped out of our sight before we saw them, but here they spun away from the craft and we only left them behind because we were still accelerating.

The second stage separated after 288 seconds: another jolt, another bang sensed through the metal of the rocket, and for a brief moment our bodies felt lighter, almost as if they were about to drift out of our seats. I saw the talisman above me tremble, seeming to dither between floating and swinging, but then the third stage fired and tremendous acceleration immediately pressed us down again. The rocket had much less mass now and this final engine set about the last part of our launch in a fierce and energetic way. G-forces rose to a respectable $3\frac{1}{2}$g. The flight was at last thrilling me with the sensation of speed.

I glanced at the on-board clock. Five hundred seconds had elapsed since we lifted away from the pad. Just eight minutes ago I had been bound to the Earth's surface, now I was in space. Eight minutes ago my family had been less than a mile away from me; now we were not even on the same planet.

At 530 seconds the third stage cut out and was jettisoned. It did not happen gradually. One moment it was burning ferociously behind me, in the next it stopped completely. One moment I was being pressed hard into my seat and in the next I was not. I had been straining against the g-force without realising I had been doing so; then I stopped straining. Quite involuntarily, I said, "*Uhh!*"

Beside me, Sergei and Tolya said, "*Uhh!*"

The talisman was no longer tense against its string. It hovered by the hatch, the string snaking loosely towards it. It had suddenly become, as we had suddenly become, weightless.

My

I was now five, and still I showed no real sign of intelligence. I showed no apparent interest in things except with my toes – more especially those of my left foot. Although my natural habits were clean I could not aid myself, but in this respect my father took care of me. I used to lie on my back all the time in the kitchen or, on bright warm days, out in the garden, a little bundle of crooked muscles and twisted nerves, surrounded by a family that loved me and hoped for me and that made me part of their own warmth and humanity. I was lonely, imprisoned in a world of my own, unable to communicate with others, cut off, separated from them as though a glass wall stood between my existence and theirs, thrusting me beyond the sphere of their lives and activities. I longed to run about and play with the rest, but I was unable to break loose from my bondage.

Left Foot

y Christy Brown

Then, suddenly, it happened! In a moment everything was changed, my future life moulded into a definite shape, my mother's faith in me rewarded and her secret fear changed into open triumph.

It happened so quickly, so simply after all the years of waiting and uncertainty that I can see and feel the whole scene as if it had happened last week. It was the afternoon of a cold, grey December day. The streets outside glistened with snow; the white sparkling flakes stuck and melted on the window-panes and hung on the boughs of the trees like molten silver. The wind howled dismally, whipping up little whirling columns of snow that rose and fell at every fresh gust. And over all, the dull murky sky stretched like a dark canopy, a vast infinity of greyness.

Inside, all the family were gathered round the big kitchen fire that lit up the little room with a warm glow and made giant shadows dance on the walls and ceiling.

In a corner Mona and Paddy were sitting huddled together, a few torn school primers before them. They were writing down little sums on to an old chipped slate, using a bright piece of yellow chalk. I was close to them, propped up by a few pillows against the wall, watching.

It was the chalk that attracted me so much. It was a long, slender stick of vivid yellow. I had never seen anything like it before, and it showed up so well against the black surface of the slate that I was fascinated by it as much as if it had been a stick of gold.

Suddenly I wanted desperately to do what my sister was doing. Then – without thinking or knowing exactly what I was doing, I reached out and took the stick of chalk out of my sister's hand – *with my left foot*.

I do not know why I used my left foot to do this. It is a puzzle to many people as well as to myself, for, although I had displayed a curious interest in my toes at an early age, I had never attempted before this to use either of my feet in any way. They could have been as useless to me as were my hands. That day, however, my left foot, apparently of its own **volition**, reached out and very impolitely took the chalk out of my sister's hand.

I held it tightly between my toes, and, acting on an impulse, made a wild sort of scribble with it on the slate. Next moment I stopped, a bit dazed, surprised, looking down at the stick of yellow chalk stuck between my toes, not knowing what to do with it next, hardly knowing how it got there. Then I looked up and became aware that everyone had stopped talking and were staring at me silently. Nobody stirred. Mona, her black curls framing her chubby little face, stared at me with great big eyes and open mouth. Across the open hearth, his face lit by flames, sat my father, leaning forward, hands outspread on his knees, his

shoulders tense. I felt the sweat break out on my forehead.

My mother came in from the pantry with a steaming pot in her hand. She stopped midway between the table and the fire, feeling the tension flowing through the room. She followed their stare and saw me, in the corner. Her eyes looked from my face down to my foot, with the chalk gripped between my toes. She put down the pot.

Then she crossed over to me and knelt down beside me, as she had done so many times before.

"I'll show you what to do with it, Chris," she said, very slowly and in a queer, jerky way, her face flushed as if with some inner excitement.

Taking another piece of chalk from Mona, she hesitated, then very deliberately drew, on the floor in front of me, *the single letter 'A'*.

"Copy that," she said, looking steadily at me. "Copy it, Christy."

I couldn't.

I looked about me, looked around at the faces that were turned towards me, tense, excited faces that were at that moment frozen, immobile, eager, waiting for a miracle in their midst.

The stillness was **profound**. The room was full of flame and shadow that danced before

---

profound intense or very deep

volition by its own choice

my eyes and lulled my taut nerves into a sort of waking sleep. I could hear the sound of the water-tap dripping in the pantry, the loud ticking of the clock on the mantelshelf, and the soft hiss and crackle of the logs on the open hearth.

I tried again. I put out my foot and made a wild jerking stab with the chalk which produced a very crooked line and nothing more. Mother held the slate steady for me.

"Try again, Chris," she whispered in my ear. "Again."

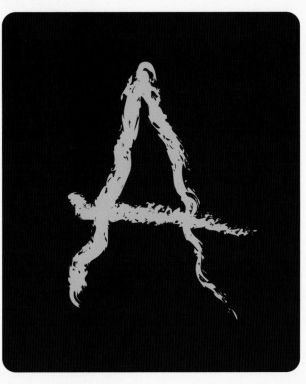

I did. I stiffened my body and put my left foot out again, for the third time. I drew one side of the letter. I drew half the other side. Then the stick of chalk broke and I was left with a stump. I wanted to fling it away and give up. Then I felt my mother's hand on my shoulder. I tried once more. Out went my foot. I shook, I sweated and strained every muscle. My hands were so tightly clenched that my fingernails bit into the flesh. I set my teeth so hard that I nearly pierced my lower lip. Everything in the room swam till the faces around me were mere patches of white. But – I drew it – *the letter 'A'*. There it was on the floor before me. Shaky, with awkward, wobbly sides and a very uneven centre line but is was the letter 'A'. I looked up. I saw my mother's face for a moment, tears on her cheeks. Then my father stooped down and hoisted me on to his shoulder.

I had done it! I had started – the thing that was to give my mind its chance of expressing itself. True, I couldn't speak with my lips, but now I would speak through something more lasting than spoken words – written words.

That one letter, scrawled on the floor with a broken bit of yellow chalk gripped between my toes, was my road to a new world, my key to mental freedom. It was to provide a source of relaxation to the tense, taut thing that was me which panted for expression behind a twisted mouth.

About the text

As part of the *Write Away* competition for young people, Darren Shan was asked to write a piece about his childhood. He chose to focus on a particular tree which became important for him.

As you read, consider the following features of the text:

Word level

- The title: why does it use quotation marks?

Sentence level

- What sort of sentence style does the writer use? Look at the use of dashes, exclamation marks and brackets.

- How does Darren Shan employ a number of poetic techniques to make his writing effective?

Text level

- How does the chattiness in style allow the writer to move in and out of the story? Is it still in chronological order?

- Can you find examples of Darren addressing the reader directly (*The next time you daydream ...*) Why does he do this?

- How does he use his own experiences to make general comments about growing up?

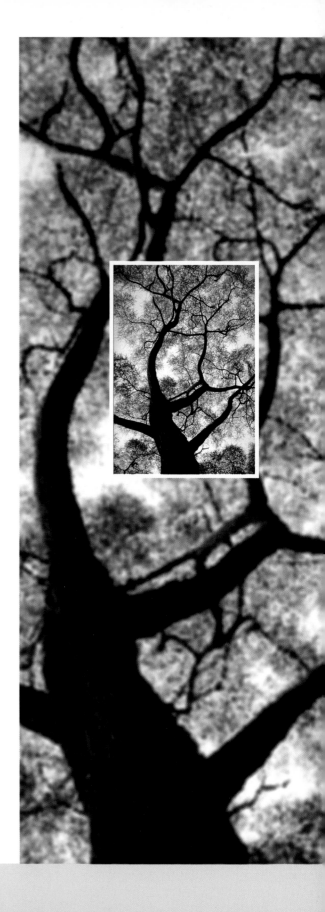

The good ship 'Tree'

by Darren Shan

When I was a kid, one of my best friends was a tree. No, I'm not a nutter! I'm not joking either. Listen: I lived in the countryside, on a road where there were no other children (except my younger brother). Most of the time I was confined to the large field out back of our house.

Television in Ireland was still in its infancy. There were two channels, and only one showed kids' programmes – a couple of hours each evening! So I (like everybody else) had to find other ways to entertain myself.

Reading, of course, was a wonderful escape, and I spent many hours locked away in a book, wide-eyed and breathless. But when I tired of reading

there wasn't much else I could do. I'd play with my brother, but he was five years younger than me – of limited appeal! I'd try making things – paper planes, catapults, bows and arrows – but DIY was never my strong suit.

Which was where the tree came in.

It was a mature plum tree. Lots of fruit in the autumn – Mum made plum jam. A great climbing tree. I spent many hours exploring the branches, figuring out how many ways I could climb up and down. I'd hang from the lower branches and time myself, then drop.

I built a treehouse: nailed several planks between the branches and constructed a rickety platform. I hung a rope from one of the planks, and tied an old tyre to the lower end – "And lo, on the eighth day, Darren invented a swing!"

The swing was fabulous. It swung around in an arc. I'd kick off from one side of the tree and circle around to the opposite side. Very fast and dangerous. If I didn't judge my re-entry just right, I'd crash into the trunk – ka-crunch!

After a while I set my imagination loose and transformed the tree and swing into – a ship! I pretended the tree was a tall ship, and the only way to power it was through the swing – the more I swung, the more power we had.

Most evenings I ran out to the tree, hopped on the swing, and spent ten or fifteen minutes 'powering up'. Once the ship was ready, I'd climb up into the 'mast' (the treehouse) and navigate. Branches became levers – if I didn't pull the right combination, all hands would be lost! I'd climb high, tug on a branch, then dash down low and yank on a twig – just avoiding an iceberg! Then I'd slide down the rope to do some more swinging, and the great cruise would continue.

I played all the crew: captain, officers, engineers, cabin boys. We raced other ships, sailed across the world, and fought off pirates. I had long conversations with myself – taking on the roles of the crew – but also with the tree. I'd bounce ideas off the bark and imagine the tree speaking back, though I knew it didn't really – as I said, I'm not a nutter!

I spent years playing out this odd but pleasant fantasy. I never told anybody about the good ship Tree – it was a secret I shared only with the plum provider. At night, when I had to leave it alone in the

perilous dangerous

was only to sit in the branches and chill out – not to sail across the globe and have **perilous** adventures.

The tree's still standing. Its branches sag now, as though tired or sad. Maybe it misses me and our fantastic voyages – or maybe its just old age!

It's been fifteen years or more since I 'sailed' the tree. Writing this has made me wonder: could I work the engines today? Could I lose myself in the fantasy again? Would the tree welcome me back as a friend and respond to my orders?

I think I'll sneak up there late tonight, when everyone's asleep. Swing on the tyre, climb up to the remains of the treehouse, whisper to the branches, "Hello, old friend." And try to set sail.

The next time you daydream, look west, to where the sea and sky meet in the horizon of the imagination. If you see a red-faced, wild-eyed guy sailing a tree, grinning like a ten year old – you'll know it's me!

dark, I'd pat its branches, salute farewell, and promise to return. I always did. Until … Actually I'm not sure when I stopped. Growing up is strange: I've stopped doing lots of things that I used to do all the time (playing with toys, watching cartoons, kicking a football against a wall), but I never remember deciding to stop. Childhood is like a habit I grew out of, unknown to myself, a bit at a time. I think that happens to most people.

Whenever and however it happened, I gradually spent less and less time up in the tree, and when I did venture up, it

About the text

How do you sum up someone's whole life in a few paragraphs? That is what the obituary writer has to be able to do. *The Daily Telegraph* is famous for its entertaining and unusual obituaries, such as the one you about to read about the life of an eccentric lion-tamer.

As you read, consider the following features of the text:

Word level

- The careful choice of verbs and adjectives keeps the writing lively.

Sentence level

- The text is written in the past tense but note the use of *would* to denote habit.

Text level

- It includes direct and indirect speech.

- It includes a number of carefully-researched facts.

- The obituary makes judgements about Jewell New, so it also offers opinions.

- It begins with his birth and ends with his death, and includes a list of those he has left behind.

Tamer who shared a motorbike with his favourite lion, Kenneth

Jewell New, who has died aged 52, excelled in persuading lions to ride motorcycles.

New took six months coaxing his favourite lion, Kenneth, to join him on his bike. "At first the cat wouldn't go near the bike," he said. "Then he wouldn't get off."

Kenneth was a mature four-and-a-half-year-old specimen when he began to learn riding pillion. New was just beginning his career and did not have enough money to buy a suitably flashy motorcycle. He had to trade in his .22 rifle and a spare tyre in part exchange. Kenneth showed a natural sense of balance as New roared round the ring, but his master sometimes complained of back strain after supporting the 30st beast's head and paws on his shoulders.

New would spend the winter months at Venice, Florida, training 15 male lions to go through their paces for a 10-minute act that he presented during the summer season for The Greatest Show on Earth, the showcase of Ringling Brothers and Barnum & Bailey. New always denied exploiting lions. "I take all the risks they do," he said.

This came home to him at a ticklish moment with another lion, Buddy. Although Buddy had been bottle-fed by New from the age of two days, he proved less tractable than Kenneth. He turned awkward at the climax of the act, when New put his head inside his jaws.

"He just kept it there," New recalled. "He didn't bite me, he just held me in place with his teeth. When he decided at last to let me go, my groom just asked me why I'd kept my head in there for such a long time." New decided in future to use a different lion for that particular trick.

Jewell New was born at Alamo, Tennessee, on October 27 1945. As a boy he picked cotton on his family's farm, and became fond of animals. While a freshman at the University of Tennessee he hitchhiked to Dallas to take a job as a keeper at the city zoo. This experience enabled him to find employment at various jungle theme parks in Texas.

New learned lion-taming by experiment, after joining Ringling Brothers' Circus World at Haines City, Florida. "The first day I asked the groom to let them in the cage with me," he remembered, "and we got acquainted. I soon figured out what I'd have to look out for."

In 1978 he took to the road for the first time with Ringling Brothers and Barnum & Bailey's 108th annual tour. He said that he felt more nervous in front of a circus audience than in a cage with a dozen Nubian lions. But his first triumph on the road seemed to him the high point of his life.

New died after retiring from the ring. He is survived by his wife Bonnie, their four sons and two daughters.

The Daily Telegraph

About the text

The following extract is the introduction to the entry for Shakespeare from World Book Online's biographical dictionary of writers (www.worldbookonline.com). It attempts to sum up the life and achievements of the world's greatest writer.

As you read, consider the following features of the text:

Word level

- The range of adjectives and adverbs used to describe the writer and his works.

- The formal language (for example, *one*, *upon*).

Sentence level

- Straightforward sentence structure designed to appeal to young readers.

- The use of past and present tenses. What effect does this have?

Text level

- Each paragraph deals with a different aspect of William Shakespeare's life and works.

- An impersonal, formal style (use of the impersonal pronoun *one*).

- The writer quotes many examples to support his arguments.

- A clear introduction and conclusion to the section.

Shakespeare, William

William Shakespeare (1564–1616) was an English playwright and poet. He is generally considered to be the greatest dramatist the world has ever known and the finest poet who has written in the English language. Shakespeare has also been the world's most popular author. No other writer's plays have been produced so many times or read so widely in so many countries.

Many reasons can be given for Shakespeare's broad appeal. But his fame basically rests on his understanding of human nature. Shakespeare understood people as few other artists have. He could see in a specific dramatic situation the qualities that relate to all human beings. He could thus create characters that have meaning beyond the time and place of his plays. Yet his characters are not symbolic figures. They are remarkably individual human beings. They struggle just as people do in real life, sometimes successfully and sometimes with painful and tragic failure.

Shakespeare wrote at least 37 plays, which have traditionally been divided into comedies, histories and tragedies. These plays contain vivid characters of all types and from many walks of life. Kings, pickpockets, drunkards, generals, hired killers, shepherds and philosophers all mingle in Shakespeare's works.

In addition to his deep understanding of human nature, Shakespeare had knowledge in a wide variety of other subjects. These subjects include music, the law, the Bible, military science, the stage, art, politics, the sea, history, hunting, woodcraft and sports. Yet as far as scholars know, Shakespeare had no professional experience in any field except the theatre.

Shakespeare was born to what today would be called middle-class parents. His birthplace was the small market town of Stratford-upon-Avon. Shortly after he married at the age of 18, Shakespeare apparently left Stratford to seek his fortune in the theatrical world of London. Within a few years, he had become one of the city's leading actors and playwrights. By 1612, when he seems to have partially retired to Stratford, Shakespeare had become England's most popular playwright.

Shakespeare has had enormous influence on culture throughout the world. His works have helped shape the literature of all English-speaking countries and of such countries as Germany and Russia. Shakespeare also contributed greatly to the development of the English language. He freely experimented with grammar and vocabulary and so helped prevent literary English from becoming fixed and artificial.

Shakespeare's influence on language has not been limited to writers and scholars. Many words and phrases from Shakespeare's plays and poems have become part of our everyday speech. They are used by millions of people who are unaware that Shakespeare created them. For example, Shakespeare originated such familiar phrases as *fair play*, *a foregone conclusion*, *catch cold* and *disgraceful conduct*. As far as scholars can tell, Shakespeare also invented such common words as *assassination*, *bump*, *eventful* and *lonely*.

Many people can identify lines and passages as Shakespeare's even though they have never seen or read one of his plays. Examples include *To be, or not to be*; *Friends, Romans, countrymen, lend me your ears* and *A horse! a horse! my kingdom for a horse!*

Shakespeare's genius as a poet enabled him to express an idea both briefly and colourfully. In his tragedy *Othello*, for example, he described jealousy as *the green-eyed monster which doth mock the meat it feeds on*. In the tragedy *King Lear*, Shakespeare described a daughter's ingratitude toward her father as *sharper than a serpent's tooth*.

Besides influencing language and literature, Shakespeare has affected other aspects of culture in the English-speaking world. His plays and poems have long been a required part of a liberal education. As a result, Shakespeare's ideas on such subjects as heroism, romantic love and the nature of tragedy have helped shape the attitudes of millions of people. His brilliant portrayals of historical figures and events have also influenced our thinking. For example, many people visualize Julius Caesar, Mark Antony, and Cleopatra as Shakespeare portrayed them, not as they have been described in history books.

Even historians themselves have been influenced by Shakespeare's greatness. Shakespeare lived in England during the reign of Queen Elizabeth I, a period known as the 'Elizabethan Age'. Historians consider the Elizabethan Age as a peak of English culture. But one can question whether the period would seem so important if Shakespeare had not lived and worked in it.

Shakespeare's widespread influence reflects his astonishing popularity. His plays have been a vital part of the theatre in the Western world since they were written more than 300 years ago. Through the years, most serious actors and actresses have considered the major roles of Shakespeare to be the supreme test of their art.

Shakespeare's plays have attracted large audiences in big, sophisticated cities and in small, rural towns. His works have been performed on the frontiers of Australia and New Zealand. They were part of the cultural life of the American Colonies and provided entertainment in the mining camps of the Old West. Today, there are theatres in England, the United States, and Canada dedicated to staging some of Shakespeare's works yearly.

Shakespeare's plays appeal to readers as well as to theatregoers. His plays – and his poems – have been reprinted and translated countless times. Indeed, a publishing industry flourishes around Shakespeare, as critics and scholars examine every aspect of the man, his writings and his influence. Each year, hundreds of books and articles appear on Shakespearean subjects. Thousands of scholars from all over the world gather in dozens of meetings annually to discuss topics related to Shakespeare. Special libraries and library collections focus upon Shakespeare. Numerous motion pictures have been made of his plays. Composers have written operas, musical comedies and instrumental works based on his stories and characters.

The world has admired and respected many great writers. But only Shakespeare has generated such varied and continuing interest – and such constant affection.

About the text

After the enormous success of the first Harry Potter book, author J.K. Rowling's life changed utterly. In this profile by the Associated Press, published in 2000 just before the publication of her next book, she is interviewed about her new life and her plans for the future of Harry Potter.

As you read, consider the following features of the text:

Word level

- Note the repeated 's' of the headline. What is this technique called, and why is it used?

- The article uses 'Harry Potter language', for example *muggles*, without explaining it. Why is this?

Sentence level

- It is written mostly in the present tense.

- J.K. Rowling's biography is dealt with in a couple of concise paragraphs in the past tense.

- The questions are either indirectly reported or implied.

Text level

- A great deal of the article consists of J.K. Rowling's own words.

- The journalist describes Rowling in a short space at the beginning and gives the reader a flavour of her personality.

- Can you work out the questions that the journalist asked but are not directly reported?

Success Stuns Harry Potter Author

by Audrey Woods

(Associated Press, 6 July 2000)

J.K. Rowling, creator of the boy wizard Harry Potter, is running a few minutes late for an interview – not quite five, in fact.

A slight figure in black trousers and a trim red-suede jacket, she slowly descends the hotel staircase, scanning the lounge for a reporter and photographer.

"Are you looking for me?" she asks, apologetic, a little flustered and far too polite to consider the obvious – that most reporters would happily wait much more than five minutes to talk with a literary phenomenon like Joanne Kathleen Rowling who up to now has revealed so little about herself.

After a quick trip upstairs, she drops her handbag onto the floor outside her suite and crouches to rummage in it for the key. "I know I have it here!"

And so she does – to the door, and to the hearts and minds of millions of children, their teachers, their parents and a lot of other adults who like her books simply because they're fun to read.

As the steadily growing band of fans knows, Harry Potter goes to Hogwarts School of Witchcraft and Wizardry and shares desperately dangerous adventures with his friends, Ron and Hermione, and a troupe of the most imaginative characters to find their way onto the printed page in years.

Rowling's transformation from struggling single mother to best-selling author is well known, and the 34-year-old's star is still ascending.

Did the creator of this magic world have the slightest inkling that so many people would take Harry to their hearts – and in 40 languages?

"Never in a million years," she says, still a bit stunned by it all and a little edgy in the days before publication of book four. She is intense and serious about her work, but down-to-earth and quick to laugh.

"Certainly, according to all the publishers that turned Harry Potter down, I was quite right in thinking that if ever it got published it was highly unlikely it would sell very many copies," she says.

"One of them felt that anything in a boarding school wouldn't sell these days," she adds with a smile. "But the one thing all of them said was it was much too long, which is kind of scary when you think that book four is over 600 pages. It even surprised me, how long it was."

Each book is longer than the previous one. And three volumes of the saga are yet to be written.

The whole series – which has sold 35 million copies worldwide – has been plotted out since 1995, when Rowling finished book one, *Harry Potter and the Philosopher's Stone*, writing in Edinburgh cafes while keeping body and soul just barely together after the failure of her marriage.

"I was incredibly skint (broke)," she says. During a Christmas visit to her sister in Edinburgh in 1993, she figured that the city was small enough so she could walk anywhere with her daughter's stroller and save the bus fare.

She had been a storyteller as a child

in western England and never really stopped, even while studying French at Exeter University and working as a bilingual secretary. She eventually went to Portugal to teach English as a second language and used her free time to work on a story about a boy wizard.

Transplanted in Edinburgh, she settled into the cafes and began bringing Harry and his friends to life.

Much of the Potter appeal lies with the cast of characters, from the loveable giant Hagrid and his baby dragon Norbert to the faceless guards of Azkaban Prison, who suck the souls out of their victims with the 'Dementors' kiss' and chill the very air in which they move.

These magic characters – and the ordinary Muggles who dwell in the parallel universe of life as we know it – were not thought up in any methodical way, Rowling explains.

"They normally come fully formed. Harry came very fully formed. I knew he was a wizard and he didn't know he was a wizard. And then it was a process of working backwards to find out how that could be, and forwards to find out what happened next."

The writing is still fun, but the latest adventure was "an absolute killer," she says, especially toward the end of the year it took to write.

"I had to be sure that that book was right because it's the central book of the seven and it's very important in plot terms ... But it was an awful lot of work," she says. "Now that I've finished, it's my favourite. It won't be to some."

Her works are not without controversy. Some parents have objected to frightening passages in previous books and to the subject of witchcraft.

Rowling says she had no wish at all to upset children but she does want to write the story her way. "I have good reason for doing it. There are certain things I want to explore and if it's the last thing I do, I will not be knocked off course."

It's a safe bet most readers like the course she's on. Initial US and British print runs of the new book total 5.3 million copies.

This level of success has changed her life, but she manages to live normally. "I see my friends, I look after my daughter – we do completely ordinary stuff," she says.

She plans to stay in Edinburgh, although the millions of dollars her books have brought could take her anywhere. And she considers one of the major pluses of her success the chance to meet young readers.

"Meeting kids who've read the books is pure, unadulterated pleasure," she says.

Rowling's respect and affection for children is almost tangible, and there is no mystery to her connection with them. But the adult readership might be harder to explain.

"I've always felt that a good book is a good book ... I never felt there was a big gulf between children's and adults' literature," she says.

Nor did she write with any plan to teach moral lessons. "I write for myself. I did not write for imaginary children: 'What would they need to learn now?'"

That goes, too, for the humour – one of the joys of the books.

"It is what I find funny," she says, "not what I think children find funny. I think it also operates on an 8-year-old level. They can read it and not get every joke and still can find most of it funny."

Rowling says that if she should ever write an adult novel, it will not be because she thinks she has to do so to be taken seriously. "I've never seen writing for children as second-best," she says.

"I am always going to be the Harry Potter author. I actually have no problem with that. I can't imagine myself ever being ashamed of these books."

③
Review and rewind

About the chapter

In this section, you will read a variety of reviews, each aimed at a different readership. In each case, there is a different 'product' (film, stage play, book and computer game), but the reviews share many features, as well as being very different in other ways.

analyse, review, comment

About the text

An enormous success in America, books by the mysterious Lemony Snicket are rapidly becoming popular in this country. You may understand why from this newspaper review.

As you read, consider the following features of the text:

Word level

- Lemony Snicket often uses old-fashioned words in his books. How does the reviewer copy this style in her review?

Sentence level

- The review uses a great variety of connectives to guide the reader from one sentence to the next.

- How is the review aimed directly at the reader? (Look at the use of the word *you*.)

Text level

- The review cleverly tells the reader the beginning of the story, and introduces us to the characters without giving the plot away.

- It begins with a quotation from the first page of the book and incorporates some of the author's words at other points.

- How does the reviewer move away from this particular book? Do we learn anything else about the author, and his other books?

- Think about how modern writers now advertise themselves (see the reference to a website at the end).

If you are interested in stories with happy endings, you would be better off reading some other book. In this book, not only is there no happy ending, there is no happy beginning and very few happy things in the middle.

So begins Lemony Snicket's well-named book, *The Bad Beginning*, the tragic tale of the Baudelaire orphans, whose lives go from bad to worse with every turn of the page.

In *The Bad Beginning* (book number one in *A Series of Unfortunate Events*), we meet Violet, Klaus, and Sunny Baudelaire, three **siblings** so clever and charming you would hate to see anything bad happen to them.

Alas, in chapter one, the Baudelaires' parents die in a mysterious fire, setting off a chain of events so hideous, so horrifying, you may prefer to follow Mr Snicket's advice by *putting the book down at once and reading something happy, if you prefer that sort of thing*.

Though their parents have left them a large fortune, the Baudelaires can't have a penny of it until fourteen-year-old Violet comes of age. This means the children have to live with a relative for the next four years, and if you're hoping they

Lemony Snicket's Deliciously Sour Tales

A review by Julia Durango

might have some sweet auntie to look after them, you're terribly mistaken.

The Baudelaires are packed off to live with Count Olaf, who is *either a third cousin four times removed, or a fourth cousin three times removed*. The only thing certain about old Olaf is that he gives new meaning to the words STINKY ROTTEN.

Count Olaf cares only about the Baudelaire fortune, and his disgusting scheme to get his greasy hands on it will make you either weep or retch. But despite the sickening circumstances, the plucky Baudelaires fight back using their unique and individual talents.

Lovely Violet is the oldest, and an engineering mastermind. Whenever she ties her hair back with a ribbon, you know she's hard at work thinking up a new invention that might just save the day.

Twelve-year-old Klaus is a bibliophile, a bookworm, a lover of libraries. In the face of danger, you can count on Klaus to put his fierce research skills to use, not to mention his vast vocabulary.

Then there's my favourite Baudelaire, young Sunny, the baby. For as much as Violet loves to invent and Klaus loves to read, darling Sunny loves to bite. With her four sharp little teeth, Sunny can bite through anything – rope, wood, ankles. Woe to the enemy who gets on the wrong side of Sunny's toothy grin!

To date, Mr Snicket has written five books in his sorrowful series (*The Bad Beginning, The Reptile Room, The Wide Window, The Miserable Mill* and *The Austere Academy*) with plans for eight more. This comes to an unlucky total of thirteen books in all.

If you've an eye for detail, and a mind for unsolved mysteries, perhaps you'll discover the secret of Beatrice along the way. Author Lemony Snicket has dedicated all of his Baudelaire books to the memory of Beatrice (*To Beatrice – darling, dearest, dead*), a beautiful young woman who seems to be intricately involved in the Baudelaire misfortunes.

And speaking of unsolved mysteries, just WHO is Lemony Snicket? At the end of each book, there's an author photo revealing only a shadowy figure, and a short, puzzling biography (*Lemony Snicket was born in a small town where the inhabitants were suspicious and prone to riot*).

Are you dying to know more? Then keep an eye out for book number six in the series, *The Ersatz Elevator*. In the meantime, check out www.LemonySnicket.com. Who knows, perhaps you'll find a new clue …

Happy reading!

siblings brothers and/or sisters

About the text

Console games are an enormous industry, and there are now a great number of magazines and websites, which cater for gamers. These are aimed at a readership that ranges in age from eight to 35, so the writers have to think very carefully about their style. Here is a review of a new game taken from a popular website.

As you read, consider the following features of the text:

Word level

- The reviewer is writing for a knowledgeable readership; what examples of gamers' jargon can you find to support this?

- The review also contains some inventive slang.

Sentence level

- The writer includes a number of poetic techniques, especially metaphor.

- There is a wide variety of sentence types including rhetorical questions. What effect do these have, and why are they used?

Text level

- The review gives the reader quite a lot of information but it is delivered in a very amusing and imaginative way.

- Look at the last sentence but one: how does this provide a satisfactory, and powerful, conclusion to the review?

Halo

It's nearly impossible to sum up Halo in a couple of short paragraphs. It's the most graphically rich first-person shooter to grace any console. It's got a robust single-player adventure and a multitude of multiplayer options. And it happens to be the most enjoyable game we've played on the Xbox thus far.

Publisher: Microsoft

XBOX ACTION GAMES

Halo takes all the elements you love about FPS games, spit-shines 'em and makes 'em sparkle! The graphics are deceiving, since you think you're looking at a PC game. With Xbox's Nvidia-born 3D accelerator, textures are photo-realistic. Grass, stone and metallic surfaces are brought to new-found heights thanks to the terrific bump-mapping.

So far, our experience with Halo has been one impressive moment after another. Shall I talk about Colin and me getting our asses handed to us by Ben and Brian in multiplayer Capture The Flag? (Colin is a terrible Warthog driver!) Should I delve into the smart, complex NPC Artificial Intelligence? At any rate, I need to find my lower jaw, which dropped off a couple of hours ago when we saw how smooth and flawless the 4-player split-screen plays.

collateral damage unintended damage to civilian property and people as a result of military activity

As a console first-person shooter, Halo's control has a slight learning curve, though it's negligible compared to other FPSs. Weapons are great and they each have a very distinct feel. The Alien Needler is the current office favourite, firing crystal shards that stick into an opponent only to explode moments after, causing spectacular **collateral damage** if used properly.

Halo is the Xbox's pride and joy. It's drenched in fun, laced with beauty and dipped in a vat of technological brilliance. If there's a shoo-in for launch, this is it.

About the text

Shrek is a good example of the excellent animated films which have been made possible by the invention of computer graphics. This review comes from Iofilm, a website that reviews films from a British perspective. The reviewer rejoices in the name of Ferret!

As you read, consider the following features of the text:

Word level

- The imaginative use of fairytale language.

- A chatty style which uses slang terms.

Sentence level

- Notice the paragraph openings, especially *Wonderful and witty …* The use of adjectives such as these at the start of a sentence is a very useful construction to use in your own writing.

Text level

- How does the writer use fairytale conventions to give the writing style? (Look at how it begins.)

- Note that the writer expects the reader to have some cinematic knowledge and so feels free to refer to other films and actors. Who do you think the review is aimed at?

Shrek

Director: Andrew Adamson, Vicky Jenson

Writer: Ted Elliott, based on the book by William Steig

Stars: Mike Myers, Eddie Murphy, Cameron Diaz, John Lithgow, Vincent Cassel, Peter Dennis, Jim Cummings

Certificate: U

Running time: 90 minutes

Made: US 2001

True romance blossoms

Once upon a time there was a Sad Little Reviewer. And the reason he was sad was that he had sat through *The Legend of Bagger Vance*, which made The Sad Little Reviewer want to hurt Matt Damon physically. But that's another story. Then The Sad Little Reviewer went to see *Shrek* …

This is the story of Shrek the ogre, a creature that looks like a cross between Danny de Vito and something that just fell out of your nose. Shrek (voiced by Mike Myers, doing his Scottish thing) is upset because Lord Farquaad (John Lithgow) has evicted all the fairytale characters into his swamp, including Eddie Murphy as a smart-ass (literally) talking donkey. *(That's a big tower. We think Lord Farquaad is compensating for something.)*

Thus begins his irreverent quest to rescue the princess, slay the dragon and defeat Lord Farquaad. A task not made any easier by the Princess (Cameron Diaz) who insists on having a proper fairytale romance with her rescuer, believing him to be a handsome prince.

But true romance blossoms when Shrek discovers that this isn't your simpering Snow White-type he's rescued. Especially when he sees her lay some *Matrix* moves on Robin Hood's men in order to stop them from doing The Riverdance (trust me, this all makes sense in context).

I encourage everyone to see this film. It's the best film of its type since *The Princess Bride*. And even if you didn't like that movie, this is probably your only chance to see a film that includes scenes of breakdancing pigs, exploding birds, a donkey seducing a dragon, and Cinders bitchslapping Snow White, while, at the same time, getting in very funny digs at Disney World, WWF wrestling and even *Blind Date*.

The animation is wonderful, making *Toy Story* look like the 'Money for Nothing' video and it also boasts a fabulous and witty soundtrack featuring Smash Mouth, eels and, would you believe, John Cale???

Wonderful and witty, *Shrek* is an instant classic and far too good for children. I just want to watch it all over again to see what I missed first time out.

And so The Happy Little Reviewer lived Happily Ever After. The End.

Review by Ferret

About the text

Charles Spencer is one of our most respected newspaper theatre critics. His review of the stage version of *The Lion King* is an example of how to write a concise and entertaining review.

As you read, consider the following features of the text:

Word level

- The use of 'lion' words at the beginning and end.

- How the text is sprinkled with a great variety of adjectives.

- A mixture of formal and informal language. Note the theatrical word *pizzazz*: what do you think this means?

Sentence level

- What range of sentence starters does he use (for example, *fortunately*, *as always*)?

Text level

- At what points does the text move from the general to the specific?

- Why does the reviewer refer to his son's response to the show?

- He suggests the audience that the show might appeal to.

- He lists the outstanding performances.

- Uses figurative language (*his eyes were out on stalks*).

Animal magic

Charles Spencer reviews *The Lion King* at the Lyceum Theatre

Disney's mighty *Lion King* has roared into the West End in triumph. I was bowled over by the show when I saw the premiere in New York two years ago, and if one was going to be coldly analytical, the Broadway staging probably just has the edge when it comes to precision and sheer pizzazz.

This time, however, I watched the show with my six-year-old son, who was transfixed. His eyes were out on stalks in the great opening scene at sunrise, when the brilliantly designed giraffes, zebras, lions, antelopes and a life-size elephant come down the aisles and take their place on the stage to the mesmeric sounds of African tribal chanting.

He was scared almost under his seat when the young lion cubs, Simba and Nala, are menaced by the truly hideous cackling hyenas. And he smiled with delight at the wonderful comic routines of Timon the meercat and Pumbaa the farting warthog, a double act who might have stepped straight off the stage of a British variety show were it not for their costumes.

Adults will enjoy *The Lion King*, especially those, in the odious modern **parlance**, still in touch with their inner child. But it is a great family show, and the word great is no exaggeration.

The original animated film was touching and entertaining, with its resonant, Hamlet-like

> **parlance** a particular way of speaking

story of a young lion growing up, avenging his father and seeing off a wicked uncle. But, like most Disney cartoons, there was a touch of the cutes about it all, and everything seemed a little too slick and glib.

The triumph of Julie Taymor's often inspirational staging is that she constantly stimulates the imagination. Throughout this show about animals, you are aware of the humans inside the ingenious costumes, and the humanity of the narrative.

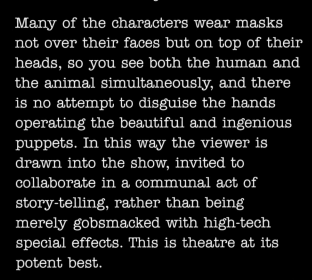

Many of the characters wear masks not over their faces but on top of their heads, so you see both the human and the animal simultaneously, and there is no attempt to disguise the hands operating the beautiful and ingenious puppets. In this way the viewer is drawn into the show, invited to collaborate in a communal act of story-telling, rather than being merely gobsmacked with high-tech special effects. This is theatre at its potent best.

The score is one of the finest in years. The pop songs by Elton John and Tim Rice are tuneful and witty, but it would all seem a touch bland if that's all *The Lion King* had to offer. Fortunately the African composer

Lebo M has added superbly haunting chants and vocal arrangements that combine Zulu tradition with the vibe of the South African townships.

The result is that the show is distinctively African, with a strong sense of place and ritual, and when the adult Simba comes to reclaim the Pridelands, it is impossible not to be reminded of Nelson Mandela.

As always with Disney, there are moments when it all seems a bit twee, others when it is excessively PC. But the ingenuity of Taymor's direction and costume designs, the beautiful, simple settings by Richard Hudson, the power of the narrative and the wit of the dialogue (Roger Allers and Irene Mecchi are responsible for the excellent book) easily outweigh such critical niggles.

Among the cast, Cornell John makes a massively dignified Mufasa and his scenes with his young son, Simba (the delightful Luke Youngblood), provide the show's emotional heart. Rob Edwards is wonderfully camp and menacing as the villain of the piece, Scar, Josette Bushell-Mingo is enchanting as the witch-doctor Rafiki, and Simon Gregor and Martyn Ellis are a riot as the meercat and warthog.

For once a mega musical lives up to the hype. This is a dazzling show with the heart of a lion.

The Daily Telegraph
Thursday 21 October 1999

④

Inside laughter

About the chapter

In this section, you will read a variety of funny pieces of writing. All except one of them is American. As you read, you might think about what makes them obviously American. Is there an American style of humour – or should that be humor?

imagine, explore, entertain

About the text

This magazine article does all the things that a guide or instructional text ought not to do!

As you read, consider the following features of the text:

Word level

- Can you identify words and phrases that are specifically American?

- What examples of formal and informal vocabulary are there?

Sentence level

- Which sentences could have come from a serious instructional text, such as a recipe?

- Some of the sentences sound angry or impatient. How does the writer achieve this?

- Many phrases are repeated. Is there a reason for this?

Text level

- How does David Neilsen make the reader believe that he really is talking to a complete idiot?

- The text works best when read aloud. Why is this?

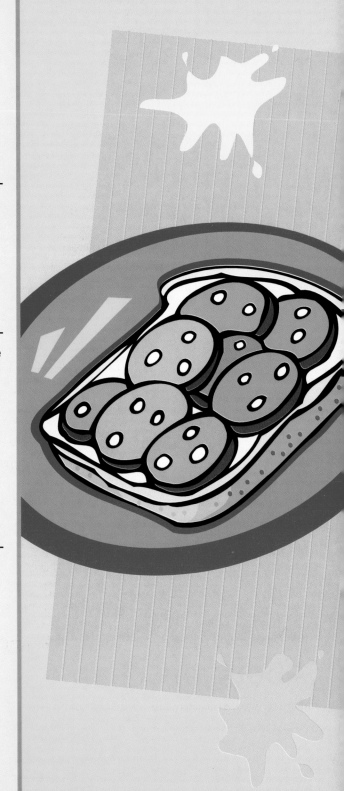

The Complete and Utter Idiot's Guide to Making a Baloney Sandwich

by David Neilsen

Hello. Welcome to The Complete and Utter Idiot's Guide to Making a **Baloney** and Cheese Sandwich. Ready for Lunch? Good! Let's begin!

We're going to start our journey by assuming that you already possess each of the individual items you'll be needing to make this sandwich. It's a bit of a stretch, I know, but Lord knows we don't have time to take you shopping.

So, that said, the first thing you're gonna need is a place to make your sandwich. My suggestion would be a plate. So reach into your cupboard and grab a plate. Any will do. No, that's a bowl. Plates are flat. Right, yes, that's flat, but it's a cutting board. Plates are going to be round. Yes the bowl is round, but it's not flat, is it? Just ... Christ, forget it. Grab that cutting board you had in your hands. Perfect. Put it down.

On the counter, not the floor.

Much better. Alright, you're ready to start. You need bread.

Personally, I prefer either wheat or sourdough, but you might prefer white, rye, pumpernickel, a French roll ... you're just staring at me. What do you mean you don't have any bread like that? Like what? What kind of bread do you have?

Wonder. Fine, it's pre-sliced.

Take out two slices of Wonder Bread. Two. More than one, less than three. That's three. Put one back. Perfect. Place your two slices of Wonder Bread on your cutting board. See how easy this is?

OK, you need some sandwich ingredients, open your refrigerator.

Your refrigerator. Big thing in your kitchen. Stores food. Yes, and beer, too. That's the one.

baloney a type of sausage

Take out the cheese, the baloney, the mayo ... you're giving me that look again. Let's stop there. Cheese, baloney and mayo. Mayonnaise. It's a sandwich spread. White. No, that's Miracle Whip. Yes, it's a white sandwich spread but ... fine. Miracle Whip will do. Put it on the counter next to the bread.

OK. Now we ... where's the cheese and baloney? Didn't I just say ... ugh! Go back to the refrigerator and ... no, leave the Miracle Whip where it is, just go back to the fridge and open it. Good. Grab the cheese. Any kind will do. Oh Jesus, just pick one!

No, that's brie. It doesn't go well with baloney. What the Hell are you doing with brie?

How about cheddar, do you have cheddar? It's probably orange. Yes! That's cheddar! Bring it to the counter next to the cutting board. Now go back to the fridge. I'm sorry, are you getting dizzy? It can happen, get used to it. Open the fridge again. You're looking for baloney. God willing, it'll be pre-sliced. Baloney. It's meat. You're looking for a package filled with slices of meat.

That's bacon.

Yes! That's the baloney! Very good! Now bring that over to the food. No, we're done with the fridge, you'll just throw out whatever you don't use, I can't bear to go through the fridge disaster again.

OK, now you're ready to start making a baloney and cheese sandwich. Open the Miracle Whip. Open it. Twist the lid off of the jar. What do you mean it won't come off? Twist the other direction. There ya go! Now you need a knife.

Oh God.

You don't need a sharp knife, you just need a spreading knife. Dull. Very dull. The duller the better. No! Not that! Put that down before you kill someone! Try to find a knife without a wooden handle. No, that has a wooden handle doesn't it? That probably means it's sharp. Don't test it to see! Just put it down! Find a dull, regular, boring knife!

OK. Perfect. That's a nice simple spreading knife. Dip it into the Miracle Whip. Now lift it out of the Miracle Whip and spread it on the slices of bread. Carefully. Not too hard, you'll tear the bread.

Harder than that. The knife has to at least touch the bread to leave the spread.

There ya go. Now do the other slice of bread. Perfect! You're a regular Julia Childs now!

She's a famous cook ... never mind.

Now your bread is spread. Quit giggling. You are going to place a slice of baloney on one piece of bread. Open the package. No, this package doesn't screw open. Just pull the back end away from the rest of the package. See how it's opening up? Excellent. Take out a slice of baloney. Place it on one of the slices of bread. No, you don't need the knife for this.

Good! You're almost there! Now it's time to cut the cheese.

I said stop giggling.

The cheese is unopened? OK, don't panic. Take the dull knife ... the other end, grab the other end of the knife! Slice the package of cheese open. Just jam it in there and ... don't worry about hurting the cheese! Just slice the damn thing open!

Very good, you're getting to be really good with the knife. Lord help us all.

Now take the block of cheese out and lay it on the counter. Just lay it on the counter, who cares if it's dirty! Like you're gonna be living long at this rate anyway! OK. Again with the knife, cut yourself a few slices of cheese. Thinner than that, you want more than two slices out of your block. Thinner. Thinner. Thinner! Just ... measure with your pinky! Your pinky should be at least two slices thick. What are you ... DON'T SLICE YOUR PINKY!!! God!

You know what? Forget it! Throw the cheese away. Throw it away! You're just having a baloney sandwich today, I can't deal with this. Don't look at me like that, throw the cheese in the garbage!

Now pick up one slice of bread and put it down on the other. Miracle Whip-side down. Well turn it over, you can't eat a sandwich with the Miracle Whip side facing out!

Because I said so!!!

OK. Pick up the sandwich.

Congratulations! You've made a Baloney Sandwich! Dufus.

About the text

The following extract is taken from Bill Bryson's extremely popular travel book, *The Lost Continent*. In this passage he describes his first impressions of Las Vegas. Although he casts a humorous eye on the city, he also has some serious points to make.

As you read, consider the following features of the text:

Word level

• Because Bill Bryson is trying to describe the scene to a reader who has probably never visited Las Vegas, he has to make the writing as vivid as possible. How is this reflected in his choice of words (for example, *Jell-O'd*, *thunk*, *clattering*) and other descriptive phrases?

Sentence level

• The author sometimes uses dashes to punctuate sentences. What effect does this have?

• What effect does the varied sentence structure have? (For example, mixing long and short sentences.)

Text level

• How does Bill Bryson create a style which is quite chatty (for example, look for phrases such as *ordinary folks like you and me*)?

• How does Bill move between some humorous comments (for example, he implies that coming from Iowa he is rather unsophisticated) and more serious points (what does he say about the woman at the end of the passage)?

Las Vegas

I got to Las Vegas and my unease vanished. I was dazzled. It's impossible not to be. It was late afternoon, the sun was low, the temperature was in the high eighties, and the Strip was already thronged with happy vacationers in nice clean clothes, their pockets visibly bulging with money, strolling along in front of casinos the size of airport terminals. It all looked fun and oddly wholesome. I had expected it to be nothing but hookers and high rollers in stretched Cadillacs, the sort of people who wear white leather shoes and drape their jackets over their shoulders, but these were just ordinary folks like you and me, people who wear a lot of nylon and Velcro.

The names on the hotels and casinos were eerily familiar: Caesar's Palace, the Dunes, the Sands, the Desert Inn. What most surprised me – what most surprises most people – is how many vacant lots there were. Here and there among the throbbing **monoliths** there were quarter-mile squares of silent desert, little pockets of dark calm, just waiting to be developed. When you have been to one or two casinos and seen how the money just pours into them, like gravel off a dump truck,

monolith a large block of stone, or something resembling that

it is hard to believe that there could be enough spare cash in the world to feed still more of them, yet more are being built all the time. The greed of mankind is practically insatiable, mine included.

I went to Caesar's Palace. It is set well back from the street, but I was conveyed in on a moving sidewalk, which rather impressed me. Inside the air was thick with unreality. The décor was supposed to be like a Roman temple or something. Statues of Roman gladiators and statesmen were scattered around the place and all the cigarette girls and ladies who gave change were dressed in skimpy togas, even if they were old and overweight, which most of them were, so their thighs wobbled as they walked. It was

like watching moving Jell-O. I wandered through halls full of people intent on losing money – endlessly, single-mindedly feeding coins into slot machines or watching the clattering dance of a steel ball on a roulette wheel or playing games of blackjack that had no start or finish but were just continuous, like time. It all has a monotonous, yet anxious rhythm. There was no sense of pleasure or fun. I never saw anyone talking to anyone else, except to order a drink or cash some money. The noise was intense – the crank of one-armed bandits, the spinning of thousands of wheels, the din of clattering coins when a machine paid out. A change lady Jell-O'd past and I got $10 worth of quarters from her. I put one in a one-armed bandit – I had never done this before; I'm from Iowa – pulled the handle

vestal virgin a Roman priestess

and watched the wheels spin and thunk into place one by one. There was a tiny pause and then the machine spat six quarters into the pay-out bucket. I was hooked. I fed in more quarters. Sometimes I would lose and I would put in more quarters. Sometimes the machine would spit me back some quarters and I would put those in as well. After about five minutes I had no quarters left. I flagged down another ample-hipped **vestal virgin** and got $10 more. This time I won $12 worth of quarters straight off. It made a lot of noise. I looked around proudly, but no one paid any attention to me. Then I won $5 more. Hey, this is all right, I thought. I put all my quarters in a little plastic bucket that said Caesar's Palace on it. There seemed to be an awful lot of them, gleaming up at me, but in about twenty minutes the bucket was empty. I went and got another $10 worth of quarters, and started feeding them in. I won some and lost some. I was beginning to realise that there was a certain pattern to it: for every four quarters I put in, I would on average get three back,

sometimes in a bunch, sometimes in dribbles. My right arm began to ache a little. It was boring really, pulling the handle over and over, watching the wheels spin and thunk, thunk, thunk, spin and thunk, thunk, thunk. With my last quarter I won $3 worth of quarters, and was mildly disappointed because I had been hoping to go for dinner and now here I had a mittful of quarters again. So I dutifully fed the quarters into the machine and won some more money. This really was getting tiresome. Finally, after about thirty minutes, I got rid of the last quarter and was able to go and look for a restaurant.

On the way out my attention was caught by a machine making a lot of noise. A woman had just won $600. For ninety seconds the machine just poured out money, a waterfall of silver. When it stopped, the woman regarded the pile without pleasure and began feeding it back into the machine. I felt sorry for her. It was going to take her all night to get rid of that kind of money.

About the text

This parody was published by the IFLA (the International Federation of Library Associations and Institutions), which is the global voice of the library and information profession. The librarians were obviously so fed up with everyone telling them that computers are so wonderful, they invented … the BOOK!

As you read, consider the following features of the text:

Word level

- This writer is having fun with words – look at all the fake (and real) technical jargon. Which are your favourite made-up phrases or words?

Sentence level

- How does the writer use the sentence structure of an explanation? Think about the use of 'signposts' such as *Here's how it works*.

- Note the occasional use of the passive voice. What effect does this have?

Text level

- The text is structured around a series of strong statements supported by evidence.

- How is the act of reading described?

- How does the final paragraph round off the text, and also point towards other 'products'?

Announcing the new built-in orderly organised knowledge device, otherwise known as the BOOK!

It's a revolutionary breakthrough in technology: no wires, no electric circuits, no batteries, nothing to be connected or switched on. It's so easy to use even a child can operate it. Just lift its cover. Compact and portable, it can be used anywhere – even sitting in an armchair by the fire – yet it is powerful enough to hold as much information as a CD-ROM.

Here's how it works: each BOOK is constructed of sequentially-numbered sheets of paper (recyclable), each capable of holding thousands of bits of information. These pages are locked together with a custom-fit device called a binder, which keeps the sheets in their correct sequence. By using both sides of each sheet, manufacturers are able to cut costs in half.

Each sheet is scanned optically, registering information directly into your brain. A flick of the finger takes you to the next sheet. The book may be taken up at any time and used by merely opening it. The 'browse' feature allows you to move instantly to any sheet, and move forward and backward as you wish. Most come with an 'index' feature, which pinpoints the exact location of any selected information for instant retrieval.

An optional 'BOOKmark' accessory allows you to open the BOOK to the exact place you left it in a previous session – even if the BOOK has been closed. BOOKmarks fit universal design standards; thus a single BOOKmark can be used in BOOKs by various manufacturers.

Portable, durable and affordable, the BOOK is the entertainment wave of the future, and many new titles are expected soon, due to the surge in popularity of its programming tool, the Portable Erasable-Nib Cryptic Intercommunication Language Stylus ...

About the text

This short piece is an example of the surreal humour of Dustin Perkins and the other contributors to *McSweeney's* magazine. It takes an everyday object and describes it in weirder and weirder ways until it becomes mysterious. You will probably never have thought of shampoo quite like this!

As you read, consider the following features of the text:

Word level

- How does Dustin Perkins take much of his language from the world of shampoo adverts?

- How does the choice of words become more poetic later in the text?

- Some phrases are clearly nonsensical (for example, *infinite constitution*) but sound good. Can you identify them?

Sentence level

- It begins with a series of questions.

- It is made up almost entirely of simple statements, one after the other. Read it aloud to see what effect this has.

Text level

- Does the writing just get sillier and sillier or are there some serious points being made?

- What joke does the writer have at the expense of the British?

SHAMPOO

by Dustin Perkins

Is your hair damaged? Is it fine and frazzled? Does it shine like it is supposed to? Does it shine like it is not supposed to? Is your hair quiet and demure or boisterous and unruly? Is it soft like silk or soft like the 'g' in 'tough'? Is your hair of appropriate length and colour for a person of your intelligence, or do you have dumb hair? Does your hair hold any degrees or certificates or is it self-taught? Is it afraid to cry?

If you answered yes or no, then you need shampoo. Shampoo is a complicated substance of infinite constitution and utility. Shampoo is supposed to make you believe that you are a part of something larger than yourself. Shampoo is a smart person that can untangle your hair's illogic. Shampoo is the most coldly rational of all the toiletries.

There is shampoo to make your hair smell like apricots, and shampoo designed to make babies cry. You need to use a lot of some shampoo, and others require you to use less. Some shampoos require that you purchase them to keep your other shampoos company, while others are merely for putting in the eyes of polite rabbits. Most shampoo is acquired by theft, and establishments, which encourage this practice, can be found in any American city.

Anything can be used to make shampoo. For example, papaya, cucumber essence, purple rain and murder would combine to make a shampoo that sells for $4.00 and comes in a purple bottle. If gold were made into shampoo it would cost $4.00 and come in a blue bottle. Some shampoo is so good that children are not allowed to buy it and people of faith regret its influence in their lives. In Great Britain, Shampoo has three 'O's and a 'U'. No one there has ever heard of it.

All types of people use shampoo. Very poor people use shampoo made of old mules and ash, and very rich people use shampoo made of poor people. Women use shampoo that smells like piña coladas. Men get important vitamins by eating that shampoo. Imaginary people use shampoo made of pure light. Dead people use shampoo that comes in a green bottle. You can only get it through the mail.

No one knows what shampoo does. No one knows where shampoo works, or how much it makes. Some people think that it makes money simply by existing in all times and places, while others think shampoo is living off an inheritance. No one knows what shampoo is or how to pronounce its name. No one has ever used shampoo or thought that it should exist. A woman once washed her hair with beer. It drove her insane.

About the text

This piece originally appeared in Mary Schmich's *Chicago Tribune* column in 1997. It takes the form of an imaginary speech that she might give to graduating American high school students.

A few years ago, the film director Baz Lurhman set it to music and it became a huge hit on both sides of the Atlantic.

As you read, consider the following features of the text:

Word level

- Because this was aimed at older students, there might be some words that you need to look up.

Sentence level

- Some sentences are only single imperative verbs (for example, *Floss*). Look at them closely; how do they come across when read aloud?

- Other sentences are simple statements addressed directly to the audience. These are often presented in pairs.

Text level

- The whole text is written in the present and future tenses. (Why are these two tenses particularly relevant?)

- The advice is a mixture of the trivial and the profound. Can you find examples as you read?

- How does Mary Schmich use humour to make some serious points?

- Do you agree with her views about young people?

Ladies and gentlemen, of the class of '97.

Wear Sunscreen.

If I could offer you only one tip for the future, sunscreen would be it.

The long-term benefits of sunscreen have been proved by scientists, whereas the rest of my advice has no basis more reliable than my own meandering experience.

I will dispense this advice now.

Enjoy the power and beauty of your youth.

Oh, never mind.

You will not understand the power and beauty of your youth until they've faded.

But trust me, in 20 years, you'll look back at photos of yourself and recall in a way you can't grasp now how much possibility lay before you and how fabulous you really looked.

You are not as fat as you imagine.

Don't worry about the future.

Or worry, but know that worrying is as effective as trying to solve an algebra equation by chewing bubble gum.

The real troubles in your life are apt to be things that never crossed your worried mind.

The kind that blindside you at 4pm on some idle Tuesday.

Do one thing every day that scares you.

Sing.

Don't be reckless with other people's hearts.

Don't put up with people who are reckless with yours.

Floss.

Don't waste your time on jealousy.

Sometimes you're ahead, sometimes you're behind.

The race is long and, in the end, it's only with yourself.

Remember compliments you receive.

Forget the insults.

If you succeed in doing this, tell me how.

Keep your old love letters.

Throw away your old bank statements.

Stretch.

Don't feel guilty if you don't know what you want to do with your life.

The most interesting people I know didn't know at 22 what they wanted to do with their lives.

Some of the most interesting 40-year-olds I know still don't.

Get plenty of calcium.

Be kind to your knees.

You'll miss them when they're gone.

Maybe you'll marry, maybe you won't.

Maybe you'll have children, maybe you won't.

Maybe you'll divorce at 40, maybe you'll dance the **funky chicken** on your 75th wedding anniversary.

Whatever you do, don't

funky chicken a novelty song and dance

Everybody's free (to wear sunscreen)

by Mary Schmich

congratulate yourself too much, or berate yourself either.

Your choices are half chance.

So are everybody else's.

Enjoy your body.

Use it every way you can.

Don't be afraid of it or of what other people think of it.

It's the greatest instrument you'll ever own.

Dance, even if you have nowhere to do it but your living room.

Read the directions, even if you don't follow them.

Do not read beauty magazines.

They will only make you feel ugly.

Get to know your parents.

You never know when they'll be gone for good.

Be nice to your siblings.

They're your best link to your past and the people most likely to stick with you in the future.

Understand that friends come and go, but with a precious few you should hold on.

Work hard to bridge the gaps in geography and lifestyle, because the older you get, the more you need the people who knew you when you were young.

Live in New York City once, but leave before it makes you hard.

Live in Northern California once, but leave before it makes you soft.

Travel.

Accept certain **inalienable** truths:

Prices will rise.

Politicians will **philander**.

You, too, will get old.

And when you do, you'll fantasise that when you were young, prices were reasonable, politicians were noble and children respected their elders.

Respect your elders.

Don't expect anyone else to support you.

Maybe you have a trust fund.

Maybe you'll have a wealthy spouse.

But you never know when either one might run out.

Don't mess too much with your hair or by the time you're 40 it will look 85.

Be careful whose advice you buy, but be patient with those who supply it.

Advice is a form of nostalgia.

Dispensing it is a way of fishing the past from the disposal, wiping it off, painting over the ugly parts and recycling it for more than it's worth.

But trust me on the sunscreen.

⑤

Teach you a lesson

About the chapter

How children are educated, and who educates them, are very important issues. In this section, you will read a variety of texts which look at these matters and, in particular, debate the question: do children learn better at home or at school?

persuade, argue, advise

About this text

As you may know, in recent years the government has found it difficult to recruit teachers. So, in order to increase the numbers of people training to be teachers, the government launched a campaign of advertisements to persuade young graduates to select teaching as a career. This is one of the advertisements.

As you read, consider the following features of the text:

Word level

- What adjectives and adverbs are used?

- What verbs and tenses are employed (for example, present and future)?

Sentence level

- Why does the writer use short sentences? Is it to make the text sound urgent and exciting? Is it easy to follow?

- Why do so many sentences start with *you*?

Text level

- Why is the text quite short?

- How does it address the concerns that it assumes people will have if they are considering teaching as a career?

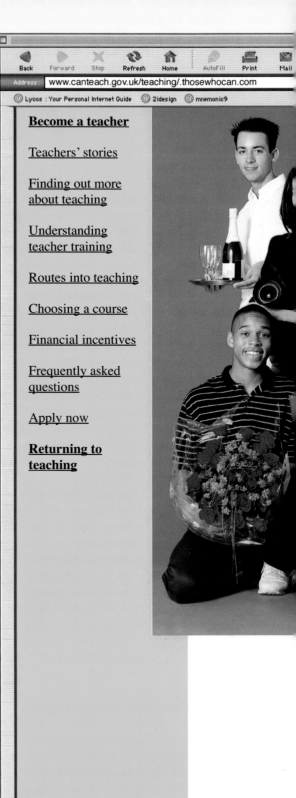

Back　Forward　Stop　Refresh　Home　AutoFill　Print　Mail

Address: www.canteach.gov.uk/teaching/.thosewhocan.com

Lycos : Your Personal Internet Guide　2idesign　mnemonic9

Become a teacher

Teachers' stories

Finding out more about teaching

Understanding teacher training

Routes into teaching

Choosing a course

Financial incentives

Frequently asked questions

Apply now

Returning to teaching

Those who can, teach

Teaching is like no other career.

It gives you the opportunity to influence young minds, to shape lives for the better. It will change your life too. You'll find it intellectually stimulating, creative and endlessly varied. Every day brings a fresh challenge.

There has never been a better time to enter teaching. Prospects are good and now the financial rewards are greatly improved too. New training salaries and other financial incentives pay you to train. Bursaries are available to many postgraduates during the training period. Starting salaries are much more attractive and, if you are good enough, you could ultimately earn more than £46,000 as a leading classroom teacher and £85,000 as a headteacher in the largest and most challenging schools.

You start with professional training designed to fit the way you live your life. There are full- or part-time courses and you can get credit for your past experience. You'll learn how to present, support, use modern multimedia tools, manage behaviour, work in teams – you'll learn how to make a difference to young people's lives. You'll soon leave behind any old notions about teaching. Opportunities quickly open in front of you, with career progression in school, a Fast Track programme and wider opportunities across a rapidly expanding education sector. You'll have the opportunity to work alongside highly skilled and committed people and the chance to develop your own knowledge and skills.

Teaching is the ultimate profession.

Because, of course, without teaching there are no other professions.

About the text

The *Sunday Times Magazine* asked a parent who had decided to educate their child at home to write a diary of their experiences. The writer is anonymous – in fact we don't even know if it is the mother or father.

As you read, consider the following features of the text:

Word level

- Note how the diary starts with quite formal language (for example, *ceremoniously*, *embark*) but that the language gradually becomes less formal.

- Why does the writer use capital letters for *The Timetable* and *The Weather*?

Sentence level

- How are brackets used in the text?

- What is the main tense used throughout the diary (except in the final paragraph)?

Text level

- It is written as a recount of the day, using temporal connectives, and often refers to the time so that we get the impression of a day passing.

- As well as telling us what happened on that day, it also makes a good case for home education.

Note: Thomas Gradgrind is a character from Charles Dickens' novel *Hard Times*. He is a very strict teacher who believes in only teaching children facts and sticking to a very rigid timetable.

4 MARCH 2001

Ellie, eight, suspects that her parents do not understand what 'proper' education involves. The night before we embark on home schooling, she ceremoniously produces a weekly timetable and sticks it on the fridge.

Just like the primary school we withdrew her from, it divides each day into Gradgrind chunks, mostly devoted to maths and language (invariably spelled 'langauge'). I focus on the fact that it also contains three 90-minute sessions of swimming, a whole morning of art, an afternoon of cooking, and only 20 minutes of RE.

Thus regulated by The Timetable, we begin our first morning of home education. At 9am, 15 minutes of touch-typing. (Ellie gets 21st-century skills; I get time for the breakfast dishes.) 9:15, 15 minutes flute practice. (Load the washing, empty the bins.) Then heads down for an hour of maths.

Diary of a home-educator

in which a parent discovers the joys and pitfalls of teaching a child at home

The first lesson is to go out – or go mad.

At 10:25 we realise that what determines our day is not The Timetable. It is The Weather. The rain is torrential. Nevertheless, we must go out, or go mad.

By the time we are sharing hot chocolate on a Starbucks' sofa, I realise that the morning has gone quite well. Ellie has sliced her way through two apples, a banana, a cake and a lot of paper to reach the dawn of understanding about what a fraction is. And I haven't needed to get cross.

Our next stop is Waterstones' floor-to-ceiling shelves of extra schoolwork for anxious parents. We reject all the English books: snippets of stories, tedious grammar. The maths books are livelier, but aimed more at homework practice than learning new skills.

Then we find Co-ordination Group Publications: Maths Classbook 3B. Its explanations make me feel like a teacher; its cartoons are from Ellie's planet. With a card game called Perfect Times, which really does teach times tables, we abandon resources-shopping and head for the library.

The library is heaven. We look up old newspapers. Ellie learns how to use a photocopier. We take home books about making musical instruments, Victorian hospitals, Matisse, **calligraphy** and little known rude facts about Shakespeare. Stuff The Timetable; this is real education.

Of course the outcome is compromise. We mix practical activities (brass rubbing, bread and butter pudding) with formal work (maths, maths, maths) and her interests (cacti, archaeology, stories with titles like Bumface). And, whatever the weather, we go out – to parks, museums, galleries, churches, nature reserves.

Cycling home at the end of one visit, we hear the shouts of children over the playground railings. "Does that make you wish you were at school?" I asked. "Not really," Ellie replied. "I miss my friends sometimes. But even though those children are in the playground, they're still behind bars."

---

calligraphy beautifully done handwriting

About the text

In this newspaper article, a journalist examines the pros and cons of home education. This is a very carefully balanced article which gives equal space to both sides of the argument.

As you read, consider the following features of the text:

Word level

- The writer uses connectives like *however* to move the reader from one point of view to the other.

- Surprisingly, the article uses the phrase *Hang on* to introduce the opposing viewpoint. It is unusual to see such an informal phrase in a text like this.

Sentence level

- Contains a large number of complex sentences punctuated by commas or dashes.

- Many paragraphs begin with an expert's name. Why is this?

Text level

- The writer has made the article livelier by basing it on the actual words of parents and experts.

- The article does not come to a conclusion.

- Sometimes the article feels like a debate. What effect does this have?

Does learning at home work?

More parents are choosing to educate their children outside school. But what are the benefits? Diana Appleyard looks at the pluses and minuses of their decision – and the role of the Internet.

by Diana Appleyard

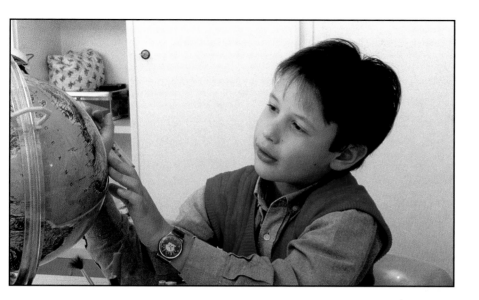

The number of parents choosing to educate their children at home in Britain is booming. The biggest organisation for home-schoolers, Education Otherwise, estimates that figures have grown from a mere handful 20 years ago to 10 000 today. The rise of home computers means that families now have much easier access to information, and since last year several British websites have been set up, dedicated to home education.

Malcolm Muckle from London set up the Education Otherwise site last September. "We've had a tremendous response from families, because in the past all of the sites have been American," he says. "Now parents here can swap information, ask for help with legal problems, discuss their children or just get in contact with each other. It means home educators don't feel so isolated, and as well as the Internet being such a ready source of information, there is also lots of excellent educational software on the market."

In America, there are now over a million home-schoolers and several hundred dedicated websites. Britain is slowly following suit.

The big question is whether home education – increasingly made more feasible by computer technology – is a sensible option for so many more children. Are parents being swept along by this trend, scared off by all the horror stories around state education?

The public perception is still that home-educated children are out of the ordinary. Mention home education, and most of us think of Ruth Lawrence, the child genius of the early Eighties who went to Oxford at the age of 12, having been intensively coached at home by her father.

Claire, who doesn't want to give her full name, educates her two children at home. She says, "I know home-educated children are seen as slightly odd, but I try not to let this worry me. I don't worry about **socialisation** at all as my children play out with other children all the time. My children also have a far greater opportunity to meet people of all ages during the day."

---

socialisation how children's behaviour changes so they fit into society

Roland Meighan is the leading light of Education Otherwise and former Professor of Education at the University of Nottingham. "Our organisation is receiving around three calls every day from parents wanting information about educating their child at home," he says. "The Home Education Advisory Service says it's providing advice to around 150 new families each month. This proves that for many parents, state education is not what they want for their children."

Meighan continues: "Parents are realising that in this country we have created more and more hostile learning conditions and **demoralised** teachers. Children are being pushed through the National Curriculum and compulsory testing. They're oppressed by the system, which doesn't encourage children to expand and develop. What is on offer in our present state school system is invalid, and children are being damaged by it."

"Hang on," says Ted Wragg, Professor of Education at the University of Exeter and a leading writer and broadcaster on education issues. "Sending your children to school is far more than just filling their heads with facts. Schools offer specialist facilities, such as gyms, labs, games fields. Good teachers mean your child is being taught by a specialist. School is vital for a child's social development, and there are also the out-of-school activities which develop a child."

Meighan counters that schools can "suck children into drugs, smoking and accepting uncritically certain styles of fashion and taste."

---

demoralised disheartened and less enthusiastic

Wragg says: "While I perfectly accept that for a few children education at home may be the best option, I would also like to raise the issue of 'separation anxiety'. We accept that many children are terrified at the thought of being separated from their parents, but there is also the concept that some parents are terrified of being separated from their children.

"They may delude themselves that their children will be somehow 'corrupted' by school, and they want to keep their children away from other people. If this is the case, I would question the motivation of these parents. The typical school is full of well-intentioned teachers and well-motivated pupils."

Katherine Thomas from Hebden Bridge in Yorkshire says her eldest son, Elliot, now six, began his educational career at the local state primary. "He managed a term and a half in reception. I'd say, 'Time to get ready for school,' and he'd say, 'I don't want to go.' It got so bad he would cry and cling on to me. He also didn't seem to be learning anything. I knew that home education was possible and legal, so I thought, 'Why not?'"

She now educates Elliot entirely at home. She will do the same with Adam, soon to be four, and 18-month-old Rebekah.

"Our approach is completely informal," she says. "I am led by the children. We talk about what they want to talk about, and I answer their questions. If it's a nice day we go out, and we visit the library and go to museums. Several times a month we get together with other home-schooling families, and we organise big outings, such as the Museum of Science and Industry.

"I don't deliberately keep track of what is going on in school, but occasionally I will get panic-stricken and think 'Elliot must know about this'. But when I try to force information on him I do tend to meet quite a lot of resistance."

Elliot tends to arrange his own day, sometimes spending several hours on his computer, surfing the Internet and using his CD-ROMs. His mother says to allocate set times for set subjects would not work for him. She says that at six, Elliot is "not really reading. His father, who works as a computer systems analyst, has designed a computer reading programme for him."

Many parents would be concerned if their child wasn't reading at six. But Meighan says: "Research has shown that home-educated children are usually two years ahead of those at school. They also have greater self-confidence, and better social skills at dealing with people of all ages."

However, for many parents, the idea of home-schooling is **anathema**. Theresa Butler, a farmer's wife from Giggleswick in Yorkshire, sends her oldest child, Anna, to the local state primary. Anna will soon be followed to school by three-year-old Rachel and baby Liam.

"I would never consider it – unless there was a really terrible reason why they couldn't cope with school," she says. "To me, school prepares them for what happens afterwards in life – the actual education is such a small part of it. They learn so many things they couldn't learn at home – such as social skills.

"I would worry that if they didn't go to school they'd get far too opinionated. They'd think they're right and that's it – they wouldn't get the skills of listening to others and discussing things."

In this country, there are now 15 Open Learning Centres, where home-educated children can meet and have group tuition. The Open School at Dartington in Devon offers home-educated children electronic courses in GCSEs via fax and email.

Online educational services, such as BT's HomeCampus, which offers all kinds of educational programmes such as homework clubs, curriculum help and links to carefully vetted websites, are ideal for home-schoolers. Access to the Internet means that children can pursue one subject they're interested in endlessly.

Meighan argues that home-educated children – because of the fact that they follow their own interests – are 'turned on' independent learners, while so many school-educated children are 'turned off' dependent learners. But because of the very fact that these children are allowed to follow their own interests most of the time, the question remains as to how they will cope with the world once they move out of their comfortable, private learning environment and whether they will ever really fit in.

anathema someone or something intensely disliked or loathed

About the text

This leaflet is produced by Parentline Plus, a UK-registered charity, which offers support to anyone parenting a child. It is designed to advise parents about ways in which they can help their children learn by supporting their education.

As you read, consider the following features of the text:

Word level

- The verbs are often imperative (for example, *help*, *encourage*) as if it is instructing the reader. However, because the article is only giving advice, the writer softens this effect by using verbs like *allow* and *let* which don't sound so bossy.

Sentence level

- What are the topic sentences in each paragraph? Look at how they are followed by additional detail or explanation. This makes each bullet point very clear.

- What examples can you find of simple statements?

Text level

- Layout is obviously very important. Look closely at the boxed text – why has this been selected?

- How does the writer or designer use a number of different font sizes and words and phrases in bold print?

Parentlineplus

helping children learn

school age children

INFORMATION SHEET 2

Parents and other family members play a vital role in supporting a child's education. Whether your child is at nursery, primary or secondary school, there is a lot you can do to help their progress.

Giving support and encouragement at home

Often, the more supported a child feels at home, the more effectively she or he will learn at school. Whatever your lifestyle, or family situation, it is never too soon (or too late) to start helping a child develop a positive attitude towards learning. Here are some ideas:

* **Give encouragement** and **show appreciation** of the child's achievements, whether great or small (e.g. making progress in reading or maths, or helping around the house). This helps to build a child's confidence.

* Help children learn that **learning can be fun** and that it can also be frustrating. Allow them to make mistakes, and to learn from them.

* Encourage a **variety of interests**, both at home, with friends, or in out of school activities..

* **Give feedback** rather than criticism: for example, by saying 'that didn't seem to work' rather than 'you got it wrong'. Again, this helps a child develop the ability to think about where they went wrong rather than feel a failure.

* **Learn together**: do things together, visit interesting places, talk about things you've seen on television, discuss life issues and give your child the opportunity to ask questions.

* Allow time for just being rather than doing. Children need time to be quiet as well as active. **Daydreaming** sometimes helps relaxation.

* Try not to ask too many questions about **homework**, especially when a child comes home from school. She or he may be tired or hungry and not feel like talking. Be available to listen later if she or he wants to talk. (See also *Information Sheet 3* in this series, *Helping With Homework*.)

* Let a child develop at his or her own pace. **Be realistic** and avoid putting your child under pressure by having over-high expectations.

* **Encourage reading** by having books, magazines and newspapers in the home and let your child see you and other family members reading them. (If reading is a problem for you, some schools have shared learning schemes which help parents and young children learn to read and write together.)

* Help children develop a **daily routine** and healthy eating patterns. Make sure they get enough sleep.

* Help children learn about **self-discipline**. Give clear guidelines about their behaviour and let them know, in a firm and gentle way, what is acceptable or unacceptable behaviour and why. Avoid giving attention only to negative behaviour as this can establish the pattern of a child doing naughty things in order to get noticed.

Taking an interest in the school

Children achieve well at school when their family and friends take an interest in their school and school work. It helps the child feel supported as well as helping to reinforce what is being learnt. Getting involved, even in the simplest way, shows your child that you care about his or her education. Parents can develop a relationship with the school by helping with activities or through the Parent Teacher Association (see *Information Sheet 4* in this series: *Families Working with Schools*).

Helping build a child's self-esteem and confidence

- Accept each child in the family for his or her own unique abilities. This helps to nurture a child's self-esteem, essential for healthy learning.

- Listen to them and praise them when they are doing something well.

- For parents of children of ethnic minorities, it is important to help a child build a positive self-image and maintain a sense of cultural identity. Try to find books, toys and games which depict people who are like you, your family and your friends and who can be seen doing a variety of jobs and activities.

- Let children learn to work things out for themselves, with your support and prompting, rather than feel you have to do all their thinking for them.

If there are problems

If your child does not seem happy at school, or seems to be struggling with school work:

- Broach the subject with the child and listen to what she or he says. She or he may have a problem with a particular subject, or a teacher, or with other pupils in the school.

- After you've talked about any problems with your child you may want to discuss them with a teacher. You have the right to ask for help in getting your child's needs met. (see *Information Sheet 4* in this series: *Families Working with Schools*).

- It may be that the child is worried or unhappy about something that is happening at home – for example, the arrival of a new baby or a family break-up. In that case, let the child know that their feelings are natural and that you understand how they feel, as well as letting the child know how you feel. (Sometimes it is easier to talk to a child away from the situation, or when things are relatively calm – when playing or doing chores together, at bed time or bath time for example.) She or he may be experiencing strong emotions, and need extra support and reassurance.

⚜ **Advisory Centre for Education (ACE)**
Tel: 020 7354 8321
Independent advice to parents of 5 – 16 year
olds on education issues in state schools
e.g. special needs, exclusion, admissions,
legal issues, bullying. Also publish 'What did
you do at school today? Understanding your
Child's Primary School'.

⚜ **Kids Club Network**
Tel: 020 7512 2112
Website: www.kidsclubs.com
For information on out of school clubs.

⚜ **Working Group Against Racism
in Children's Resources (WGARCR)**
Tel: 020 7627 4594
Information on books, toys and resources
which provide positive representation.

⚜ **'Is your child about to start school?'**
A useful leaflet published by Qualifications
and Curriculum Authority.
Tel: 020 7509 5555

⚜ **National Confederation of
Parent Teacher Associations (NCPTA)**
2 Ebbsfleet Estate, Stonebridge Road,
Gravesend, Kent DA11 9DZ
Tel: 01474 560 618
Website: www.ncpta.org.uk
Provides information on setting up Parent
Teacher Associations and developing home-
school links.

⚜ **The Letterbox Library,**
Unit 2D, Leroy House,
436 Essex Road, London N1 3QP
Tel: 020 7226 1633
A source of multicultural
and anti-sexist books.

Parentline_{plus}

Unit 520, Highgate Studios,
53-79 Highgate Road, Kentish Town,
London NW5 1TL

Email centraloffice@parentlineplus.org.uk
www.parentlineplus.org.uk

Parentline: 0808 800 2222
Textphone: 0800 783 6783

DfEE
Department for
Education and Employment

Design Origin

⑥
Let me explain

About the chapter

This section looks at the different ways that writers go about explaining complex ideas in newspapers, books and websites.

inform, explain, describe

About the text

How does a daily newspaper report a scientific innovation? In this article from *The Daily Telegraph*, the reporter takes a humorous look at a new kind of shirt.

As you read, consider the following features of the text:

Word level

- What scientific terms are used? Do these make the text too difficult to read, or are they used carefully so that the ordinary reader can understand?

Sentence level

- The writer uses straightforward connectives (for example, *when*, *because*) to keep the report simple.

- Notice the use of the present tense throughout with *has been* to denote something that happened in the past.

- Also, note the use of the passive voice.

Text level

- A very clever headline draws the reader's attention to the article.

- How is the article built around direct quotation from an expert?

- The mention of the respected journal *New Scientist* lends the report credibility.

- The report ends with a joke. In your opinion, is the text as a whole light-hearted or serious?

Smart shirt rolls up its own sleeves

by Robert Uhlig

A shirt that never needs ironing and which rolls up its own sleeves when its wearer gets too hot has been unveiled by an Italian fashion house.

Made of an **alloy** called nitinol interspersed with nylon, the shirt has a characteristic called shape memory that enables designers to incorporate several advanced features.

"The sleeve fabric is programmed to shorten as soon as the room temperature becomes a few degrees hotter," said Susan Clowes, for Corpo Nove, of Florence, the shirt's developer.

The £2,500 shirt could be a traveller's dream, *New Scientist* reports. Creases can be removed even while the shirt is being worn because the nitinol alloy returns to its original shape when heated to a certain temperature.

"Even if the fabric is screwed up into a ball, pleated and creased, a blast from a hairdryer pops it back to its former shape," Miss Clowes said. City workers are unlikely to be wearing the shirt, not least because it is available only in metallic grey.

> **alloy** a mixture of two or more metals

Special offer only £2,500!

About the text

The following web page comes from the amazing *How Stuff Works Express* website. This site attempts to explain the most difficult ideas to young people, and it has set itself a hard task. Does it succeed?

As you read, consider the following features of the text:

Word level

- The text actually uses very few technical terms, and those it does use are carefully explained.

- Some of the language is surprisingly informal.

Sentence level

- Most sentences are quite short, using *but*, *if* and *so* to connect ideas.

- The text addresses the reader directly.

- There are examples of instructional writing to help the reader build a picture in his or her head. Do these work in making the text clear?

Text level

- The layout is crucial. Look at the use of text boxes, fonts and illustrations.

- How are the paragraphs organised so the reader does not have to cope with too many ideas in one go?

- The writer uses humour, and everyday examples to help make the ideas clear.

Address: www.howstuffworks.com/time.htm

Lycos : Your Personal Internet Guide   2Ldesign   mnemonic9

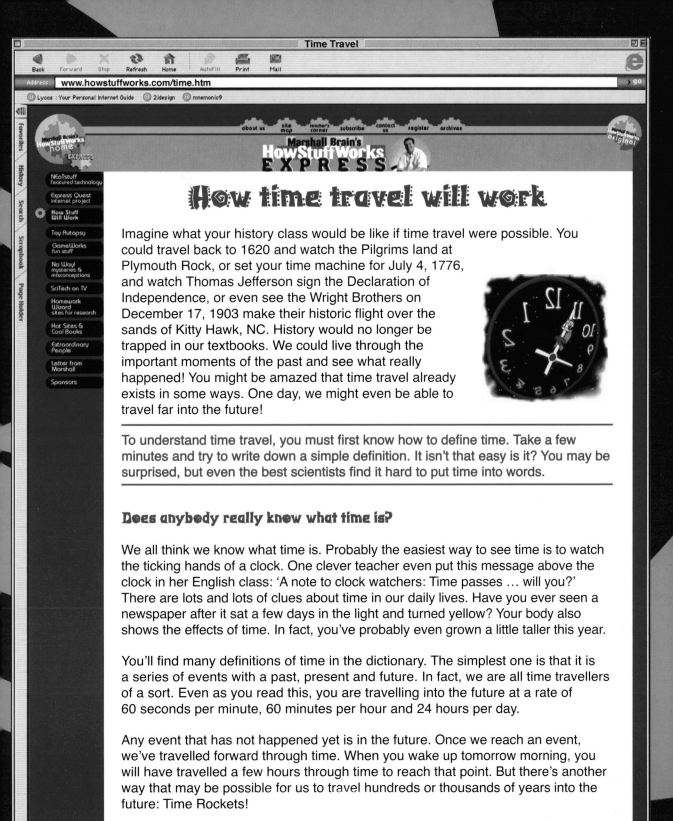

How time travel will work

Imagine what your history class would be like if time travel were possible. You could travel back to 1620 and watch the Pilgrims land at Plymouth Rock, or set your time machine for July 4, 1776, and watch Thomas Jefferson sign the Declaration of Independence, or even see the Wright Brothers on December 17, 1903 make their historic flight over the sands of Kitty Hawk, NC. History would no longer be trapped in our textbooks. We could live through the important moments of the past and see what really happened! You might be amazed that time travel already exists in some ways. One day, we might even be able to travel far into the future!

To understand time travel, you must first know how to define time. Take a few minutes and try to write down a simple definition. It isn't that easy is it? You may be surprised, but even the best scientists find it hard to put time into words.

Does anybody really know what time is?

We all think we know what time is. Probably the easiest way to see time is to watch the ticking hands of a clock. One clever teacher even put this message above the clock in her English class: 'A note to clock watchers: Time passes … will you?' There are lots and lots of clues about time in our daily lives. Have you ever seen a newspaper after it sat a few days in the light and turned yellow? Your body also shows the effects of time. In fact, you've probably even grown a little taller this year.

You'll find many definitions of time in the dictionary. The simplest one is that it is a series of events with a past, present and future. In fact, we are all time travellers of a sort. Even as you read this, you are travelling into the future at a rate of 60 seconds per minute, 60 minutes per hour and 24 hours per day.

Any event that has not happened yet is in the future. Once we reach an event, we've travelled forward through time. When you wake up tomorrow morning, you will have travelled a few hours through time to reach that point. But there's another way that may be possible for us to travel hundreds or thousands of years into the future: Time Rockets!

Lycos : Your Personal Internet Guide   2idesign   mnemonic9

Light speed time machines

The key to speeding up time travel and allowing us to jump into the future is to build vehicles that can travel at the speed of light – or at least near light speed. Light speed equals 186 000 miles per second! That is about 11 million times faster than a car travelling at 60mph! Scientists claim that time actually slows down for you as you near light speed. So, if you had a time machine that allowed you to travel at the speed of light, time would slow down for you – but it would remain the same for those not in the time machine.

But here's the hitch. Scientists don't believe that matter can actually reach the speed of light. The good news is that we don't need to travel at the speed of light to travel through time. In fact, we already have spaceships that can jump into the future.

The space shuttle travels at about 17 500 miles per hour. That's 40 000 times slower than the speed of light speed. But even at that speed, scientists calculate that astronauts aboard the space shuttle travel a few nanoseconds into the future. A nanosecond is a tiny speck of time – only a billionth of a second. It is so fast that, by the time you can blink your eye, 400 000 nanoseconds have gone by! If we could build a spaceship that is thousands of times faster than the space shuttle, then we could travel weeks or years into the future.

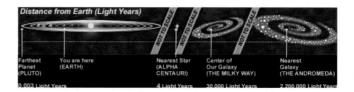

Distance from Earth (Light Years) — NOT TO SCALE
Farthest Planet (PLUTO) 0.003 Light Years; You are here (EARTH); Nearest Star (ALPHA CENTAURI) 4 Light Years; Center of Our Galaxy (THE MILKY WAY) 30,000 Light Years; Nearest Galaxy (THE ANDROMEDA) 2,200,000 Light Years

If one inch equals one light year, here's how far these celestial bodies would be from Earth: Pluto 0.003 inches; Alpha Centauri (nearest star) 4 inches; centre of the Milky Way (our galaxy) 0.5 miles; Andromeda (nearest galaxy) 35 miles.

Think about this. You and a friend want to go to Pluto, the farthest planet from the Sun. Pluto is about 3.5 billion (3 500 000 000) miles from Earth. You both want to go and see Pluto, but there is only room for one of you in the spaceship. So you go, while your friend stays behind. Let's say that your spacecraft can travel at only 324 million mph, or about half the speed of light. At that high speed, you could travel to Pluto and back in about one day. Even though you've only experienced a little less than 24 hours, your friend back on Earth would have experienced nearly two days. You travelled so fast that time slowed for you. So, in effect, you jumped about a day into the future!

Address: www.howstuffworks.com/time.htm

Tunnelling through time ...

Another way that time travel could exist is by creating a 'wrinkle in time'. There's a great book that deals with this theory, called *A Wrinkle in Time*, written by Madeleine L'Engle. In this book, a group of children travel through time and space using the fifth dimension of time travel. This novel is actually based on the idea that space can be folded in order to allow for more rapid travel. While our universe is three dimensional, imagine for a moment that it is two dimensional … like a sheet of paper.

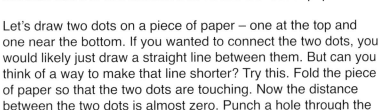

Let's draw two dots on a piece of paper – one at the top and one near the bottom. If you wanted to connect the two dots, you would likely just draw a straight line between them. But can you think of a way to make that line shorter? Try this. Fold the piece of paper so that the two dots are touching. Now the distance between the two dots is almost zero. Punch a hole through the paper where the two dots connect.

This piece of paper represents our universe and the line we've drawn is the route our spaceship would take to get from Earth to another far away planet. If we could 'fold' space, like we folded the piece of paper, then we've eliminated time and distance from our journey. That hole you punched is similar to a tunnel that would allow us to journey to planets millions of miles away in nearly no time.

Back to the future

You don't need a time machine to look into the past. Just look up at the sky. Most of the stars in the sky are trillions of miles away from Earth. Even the closest star is 25 trillion miles away. That is the number 25 followed by 12 zeros! Since light travels at 670 million miles per hour, it takes this light about 4.3 years to reach us. So, when you look up at night and see a star, what you are actually seeing is what it looked like years and years ago. You'll have to wait another 4 or 5 years to see what that star looks like right now. Some stars are so far away that it takes millions of years for their light to reach us. The Andromeda Galaxy, for instance, is the most distant object visible to the naked eye. It is 2.2 million light years away! We use the most distant stars to help "see" what happened at the beginning of the universe.

Links: **www.howstuffworks.com/time.htm**

About the text

Russell Stannard has written a series of 'Uncle Albert' books to help young children to understand complex scientific concepts. (Uncle Albert is a reference to the famous genius, Albert Einstein.) In *Letters to Uncle Albert* and its sequel *More Letters to Uncle Albert*, children have written in to him with their questions. 'Uncle Albert' replies.

As you read, consider the following features of the text:

Word level

- The vocabulary is very simple, using occasional childish words (for example, *whizzing*) to make his readers feel comfortable.

- What examples of chatty, or informal words and phrases can you find?

Sentence level

- The sentences are short, using *so*, *if* and *whereas* to connect ideas.

- Look at the beginning of each paragraph. Notice how Russell Stannard introduces his ideas.

Text level

- Presentation is very straightforward with the question reproduced in the child's own (misspelled) writing.

- The answer is concise and does not use any diagrams or layout features. Would the answers be helped by this, or do they work as they stand?

If the earth rotation has stoped and reversed would we carry on as normal or would we go back in time?

Yours sinserely

Gemma (Age 10)

No, we would not go back in time if the Earth's rotation reversed. In fact, I don't think it will ever be possible to go back in time (despite what we are told in science fiction stories and films). Playing around with these ideas can be lots of fun, but if you take them seriously you soon get into problems.

Uncle Albert

Suppose, for example, you went back in time and found yourself driving a stage coach. While worrying about how you are going to get back to the present, your mind wanders and you accidentally run over and kill your great grandmother. If that happened she would not have been able to give birth to your grandmother, who wouldn't have given birth to your mother, who wouldn't have had you. So, you couldn't have gone back in time in the first place, because you couldn't have existed in the first (or is it the last) place.

Mind you, if the Earth's rotation suddenly reversed, you would still not 'carry on as normal'. Just think: the distance round the Earth's Equator is about 40 000 kilometres. The Earth rotates once every 24 hours. So that means someone standing on the Equator is actually whizzing round through space at about 1 7800 kilometres per hour (though of course it doesn't seem like it because everything at the Equator is going at the same speed). Now, suppose the Earth suddenly stops. What's going to happen? All the loose things on the surface (people for instance) will carry on at 1 700 kilometres per hour, whereas hills and mountains won't. So the people had better watch out! And then there is all that loose stuff called seas and oceans. All that water is suddenly going to come ashore at 1 700 kilometres per hour.

I reckon it's a good thing that the Earth is likely to carry on the way it is for a long, long time!

About the text

This text is taken from an inspiring website called *Bagheera* at www.bagheera.com. It is dedicated to saving endangered species. The site devotes one section to explaining every aspect of the elephant and its life. This extract gives a flavour of its style and substance.

As you read, consider the following features of the text:

Word level

- The vocabulary is formal, giving the writing a 'textbook' feel.

- Despite its campaigning purpose, the vocabulary is quite plain and unemotional. Why might the writer have done this?

Sentence level

- The writer uses a wide variety of sentence starters, sometimes starting with an adverb. This livens up what could be a dry text.

- Generally, the writer uses a very impersonal style.

Text level

- The writer does not address the reader directly.

- How are the sections separated into different aspects?

- What is the purpose of the first section? Is it to act as a general introduction? Or to grab the attention?

- Facts and figures are used extensively. Why is this important?

Throughout history, the elephant has played an important role in human economies, religion and culture. The immense size, strength and stature of this largest living land animal has intrigued people of many cultures for hundreds of years. In Asia, elephants have served as beasts of burden in war and peace. Some civilizations have regarded elephants as gods, and they have been symbols of royalty for some. Elephants have entertained us in circuses and festivals around the world. For centuries, the elephant's massive tusks have been prized for their ivory.

The African elephant once roamed the entire continent of Africa, and the Asian elephant ranged from Syria to northern China and the islands of Indonesia. These abundant populations have been reduced to groups in scattered areas south of the Sahara and in isolated patches in India, Sri Lanka, and Southeast Asia.

Demand for ivory, combined with habitat loss from human settlement, has led to a dramatic decline in elephant populations in the last few decades. In 1930, there were between 5 and 10 million African elephants. By 1979, there were 1.3 million. In 1989, when they were added to the international list of the most endangered species, there were about 600 000 remaining, less than one percent of their original number.

Asian elephants were never as abundant as their African cousins, and today they are even more endangered than African elephants. At the turn of the century, there were an estimated 200 000 Asian elephants. Today there are probably no more than 35 000 to 40 000 left in the wild.

DESCRIPTION

At first glance, African and Asian elephants appear the same. An informed eye, however, can distinguish between the two species. An African bull elephant (adult male) can weigh as much as 14 000 to 16 000 pounds (6 300 to 7 300kg) and grow to 13 feet (4 metres) at the shoulder. Its smaller relative, the Asian elephant, averages 5 000 pounds (2 300kg) and 9 to 10 feet (3 metres) tall. The African elephant is sway-backed and has a tapering head, while the Asian elephant is hump-backed and has a huge, domed head. Probably the most interesting difference between the two species is their ears. Oddly, the African elephant's large ears match the shape of the African continent, and the Asian elephant's smaller ears match the shape of India.

Elongated incisors (front teeth), more commonly known as tusks, grow up to 7 inches (18cm) per year. All elephants have

The elephant

tusks, except for female Asian elephants. The largest of the African bulls' tusks can weigh as much as 160 pounds (73kg) and grow to 12 feet (4 metres) long. Most animals this big, however, are gone; they were the first to be killed for their ivory.

Most African elephants live on the **savanna**, but some live in forests or even deserts. Most Asian elephants live in forests. As herbivores (plant eaters), elephants consume grass, foliage, fruit, branches, twigs and tree bark. Elephants spend three-quarters of their day eating, and they eat as much as 400 pounds (180kg) of vegetation each day. For this task, they have only four teeth for chewing.

In the hot climates of their native habitats, elephants need about 50 gallons (190 litres) of water to drink every day. Elephants boast the largest nose in the world, which is actually part nose and part upper lip. It is a large natural hose, with a six-gallon (23-litre) capacity.

under the leadership of an older female or matriarch. Adult males are solitary, although they stay in contact with the females over great distances, using sounds well below the range of human hearing. Family groups communicate with each other using these low-frequency vibrations. It is an eerie sight to see several groups converging on a waterhole from miles apart, apparently by some prearranged signal, when human observers have heard nothing.

The natural lifespan of an elephant, about 70 years, is comparable to a human's. Elephants reach breeding age at about 15 years of age. Females generally give birth to one 200-pound baby after a 22-month pregnancy.

ELEPHANTS AND HUMANS

Humans first tamed Asian elephants more than 4 000 years ago. In the past, humans used elephants in war. Elephants have been called the 'predecessors to the tank' because of their immense size and strength. They were important to military supply lines as recently as the Vietnam War in the 1960s. Although African elephants are harder to train than Asian, they too have worked for humans, mostly during wartime. For example, the elephants that carried Hannibal's troops across the Alps to attack the Romans in 200 BC were African.

In modern times humans use elephants primarily for heavy jobs like hauling logs. An elephant is the ultimate off-road vehicle and can get tremendous traction even on slippery mud. An elephant actually walks on its toes, aided by a great flesh heel-pad that can conform to the ground.

In some remote areas of Southeast Asia it is still more economical to use elephants for work than it is to use modern machinery. Scientific researchers use elephants for transportation in the hard-to-reach, swampy areas they study, and tourists ride elephants to view wildlife in Asian reserves. Elephants are the ideal mobile viewing platform in the tall grass found in many parks.

Asia has always had a strong cultural connection to the elephant. In Chinese, the phrase 'to ride an elephant' sounds the same as the word for happiness. When Thailand was called Siam, the sacred White Elephant dominated the flag and culture. According to Thai legend, in the beginning all elephants were white and flew through the air, like the clouds and rain. Thousands of years later, a white elephant entered the side of Queen Sirimahamaya as she lay sleeping. Later she gave birth to Prince Siddhartha, the future Guatama Buddha. Among the **predominantly** Buddhist kingdoms of Southeast Asia, the most **auspicious** event possible during a monarch's reign was the finding of a white elephant.

---

auspicious favourable

predominantly chief or main

⑦ Hear my voice

About the chapter

In this section, you will be able to compare the different ways in which writers try to persuade us to take their point of view. In most cases, these views are part of larger campaigns, or national action on specific issues.

persuade, argue, advise

About the text

The future of foxhunting in this country has been the subject of debate for a long time. Over the past few years, anti-hunt campaigners have taken to sabotaging hunts to save the foxes and win publicity for their cause. This leaflet was produced by a group of hunt saboteurs.

As you read, consider the following features of the text:

Word level

- The writer includes a large number of powerful and emotive words to persuade the reader. Can you identify them?

Sentence level

- The leaflet begins in the present tense to make it more dramatic.

- The sentence starters also add to the drama (*To my amazement* ... , *Grabbing* ...).

- The bulk of the text is in the saboteur's own words. What is the effect of this?

Text level

- The picture and caption make us want to read on.

- Although most of the text is taken up with Copper's story, can you see the broader point the writer is trying to make?

West Sussex. Saturday, 6th February 1999. Around 1pm the hounds of the Chiddingfold, Leconfield and Cowdray Foxhunt scent a fox and give chase. When they finally bear down on the exhausted animal, only eighteen months old and the size of a terrier, it is no match for the hounds. Luckily, Andy, a local hunt saboteur is also there ...

"When I saw the hounds bite into the fox's backside, I knew I had to do something and the only thing left was to jump in and rescue the fox myself. Grabbing the fox distracted the hounds enough for them to let it go, but the terrified fox bit me and I lost my hold ... the fox saw its chance and bolted down a rabbit burrow. Its tail was still poking out, so I sat on the hole to stop the hounds from snapping at it. To my amazement, a policeman lent me his helmet to plug the hole, and refused to let the hunt dig out the fox and kill it. Even the police must have been affected by the plight of this pathetic little creature! Eventually, once the hunt had left, we got the fox into a travelling cage and raced it to the vet's."

'Copper', irreverently named after the policeman who helped in the rescue, was examined by wildlife vet, Richard Edwards, who said the fox would have died without prompt treatment. However, its life-threatening condition was not caused by the bites Copper had received, but by extreme stress – caused by the prolonged chase of the hunt. (He had even begun to bleed from his penis, evidence of kidney damage due to trauma or extreme physical exhaustion.) After medical treatment, Copper spent some weeks recovering and recuperating in a wildlife hospital. He was released, fit and well, into a non-hunting area in March 1999.

Copper's case explodes the myth that a hunted fox is either killed 'by a quick nip to the back of the neck' or gets away. The bite marks to Copper's hind legs – and Andy's eye-witness account – show that hounds will snap at any part of a hunted fox to bring it down.

His general condition is proof that, as in the case of hunted stags (highlighted in the 1997 Bateson Report), hunted foxes suffer intolerable levels of stress as a direct result of the chase itself. The hunting **fraternity** have always known this. In 1960, Lord Paget wrote: "Pain and suffering is inflicted on animals in the name of sport. Nobody who has seen a beaten fox dragging his stiff limbs into the ditch in which he knows he will soon die, can doubt this proposition."

That's why, although Copper's rescue was successful, Andy doesn't consider February 6th a good day's sabbing. "For us a good day is one where the hunt don't get to chase an animal at all," he explains. Covering scent with a mixture of water and citronella oil, or using horn calls to draw the hounds away from a hunted animal are both tactics used by saboteurs to stop a chase before it even begins! Until hunting is banned, the only chance animals like Copper have to evade a cruel and terrifying death, is people like Andy …

'COPPER'

LIVING PROOF

THAT HUNT SABOTEURS SAVE LIVES

fraternity a group of people with similar interests

About the text

Many people, especially those who live in the countryside, enjoy foxhunting. Pro-hunting campaigners can't really use the same campaigning techniques though. Here is an article from *The Guardian* newspaper in which an anonymous hunter makes his or her case.

As you read, consider the following features of the text:

Word level

- Unlike the previous example, this text is very matter-of-fact, employing few adjectives.

Sentence level

- The sentence structure is much closer to an information or explanation text. What effect might this have on the reader?

Text level

- This article also tells a story but it is very different in tone from 'Copper'.

- The language sounds very reasonable and calm.

A JOB HAS BEEN DONE FOR THE FARMER

from The Guardian, *Monday 11 October 1999*

Hunting is, amongst many other things, a community event. At the meet, which typically takes place at a farmhouse at 11am, riders, horses, followers on foot and by car, hounds and hunt workers gather to start the day. Rural life can be very isolating, and hunting brings together people from a broad cross-section of the community, where views on a whole range of countryside and other issues are exchanged.

The huntsman – a hunt employee in charge of the hounds during the day's hunting – leads them away from the meet and to the first 'draw', which will typically be a 'covert' (wood) or hedge-line. A pack typically consists of 21 'couples' of hounds (i.e. 42 dogs). They work naturally together as a pack and use their noses to seek the scent of a fox. Like all dogs, hounds hunt naturally, but foxhounds are trained to only hunt the fox and to follow the instructions of the huntsman, given by voice or by blowing a horn.

If the hounds detect a fox's scent or indeed flush one from the woodland, they 'speak' (a distinctive barking) and will hunt the fox by following its scent. According to research by Oxford University fox expert Dr David Macdonald, the average hunt of each fox lasts for 17 minutes. This does not, however, involve the fox running flat out with the hounds at his heels. He is likely to be some distance ahead for most of the hunt, unable to see the hounds, but aware there is a danger and moving away from it.

A fit fox will frequently escape, but the ageing, injured or diseased animal is far less likely to be able to outrun the hounds. As such, hunting is the only form of fox control that employs natural selection, picking out those animals most in need of **culling**, and also most likely to be a pest to the farmer.

The riders follow the pursuit behind the hounds, the huntsman and a 'field master' who decides which route they follow. Hunting provides a unique excitement, following an unpredictable quarry across country, jumping obstacles such as hedges and gates as they present themselves. Others follow the chase on foot, bike or by road, enjoying trying to keep up with the progress of the hunt and watching the hounds 'working' (following the scent).

All these followers are essential to the hunt, as their subscriptions help fund the maintenance of the hunt kennels, the care of hunt horses and hounds, and the employment of the huntsman and other workers. In return for the hunt's contribution to

culling reducing the size of a group of animals by selective killing

the management of the fox population, farmers allow the followers access to their land – a successful form of **symbiosis**.

If the hounds catch the fox, its death is very quick. A foxhound weighs around five times as much as a fox, and the first hound to reach the fox typically kills it with a powerful bite, breaking its neck. As with most predators, the hound is designed to kill its prey as swiftly as possible. Hunting guarantees a fox is either killed outright or escapes unharmed.

Sometimes a fox will elude hounds by going down a hole. if the farmer requires it, a hunt employee who is licensed will send in a terrier to bring the fox 'to bay' (where terrier and fox stand their ground facing each other). The 'terrierman' will then dig down to where the terrier is barking and shoots the fox swiftly at point-blank range, using a 'humane killer' – a form of pistol used to put down animals.

Hunting takes place several days a week for most of the 300 UK packs, and each day's hunting consists of a number of individual hunts as described above. Each is unique, which is another attraction of the sport. There are 22 500 hunting days in the UK each year.

The day ends back at the meet, with both followers and horses tired after an exhilarating day. Although one or more foxes are likely to have been killed, it is unlikely that most followers will have seen it happen, and that's not why they go. But they all recognise that a job has been done for the farmer, and that this is the only reason they have enjoyed such unrivalled access to private land.

symbiosis two animal or plant species living closely and depending on each other

About the text

Frank Furedi wants us to change the way that our society brings up children. He believes that children are being prevented from learning important lessons about growing up because they are no longer allowed out to play on their own. He has written a book on this subject and in this newspaper article, he puts forward his point of view.

As you read, consider the following features of the text:

Word level

- The writer uses *we* in the article to include his reader.

Sentence level

- The article moves between the past and present tenses.

- Each paragraph begins with an attention-grabbing topic sentence. Are there any particularly good examples of this?

Text level

- This article gives no space to an opposing view. It assumes that the reader agrees with its point of view.

- Frank Furedi uses university research as evidence. How does this help his argument?

Accidents should happen

Parents' irrational fears are damaging children, says sociologist Frank Furedi in his controversial new book, Paranoid Parenting. *Here, he asks what happened to playing outdoors.*

When I was a child, I loved the day the clocks went forward – it meant evenings would be lighter, giving us more time to play outside after school. It also meant that warmer weather would be on the way and that meant that my friends and I could escape from under our parents' feet and have fun or, as they saw it, get up to mischief.

Like *The Fast Show's* Ron Manager, we all remember jumpers for goalposts. But school ties came in handy, too, being used for binding the hands of boys 'taken prisoner' in play raids. School shirts were stained green from lying on grass. By the time the Easter holidays came, we were never at home. We were far too busy lugging perilously large objects into trees and bushes to make 'camps', from which we could launch attacks on other children.

These days, it's rare for children to spend time like this, without the company of adults, making and breaking their own rules in their own games. Today, we worry that, left unsupervised, children will fall victim to all manner of risks it is our duty to prevent. The obsession with child safety is so dominant that even the sources of spontaneous outdoor fun of a decade ago are being taken away.

litigious excessively ready to go to law

Take something as apparently harmless as conkers, a game that has probably been an accepted part of children's play since the invention of string. Well, possibly not for much longer. While researching the growth of compensation culture in Britain, I recently learned that some local authorities were so worried that they might be sued by parents of children injured conkering that they had implemented a policy of 'tree management' to make horse-chestnut trees less accessible to children.

And it gets worse. A recently published survey by Sarah Thomson, a researcher at Keele University, indicates that it is not just local authorities that are out to ban conkering. Schools, too, are banning such traditional playtime games because headteachers are anxious about being sued by **litigious** parents. Thomson claims that some schools have banned conkers because they fear a chestnut on a string could be used as an 'offensive weapon'.

It is not only the school playground that has become a focus of the obsession with child safety. A wave of anxiety about children's safety outdoors threatens to turn the traditional public playground (the 'rec') into an endangered species. Much-loved fixtures such as monkey bars and merry-go-rounds are soon to be consigned to the museum. Fixed goalposts are being removed. Witches' hats and the plank swing have been banished. New roundabouts are smaller and slower and, of course, the swings are shorter. One accident in a playground can lead to the permanent closure of an amenity. In Greenwich, south London, five playgrounds were shut following an incident in which a single child was injured.

The attempt to transform playgrounds into risk-free zones coincides with a more general pattern. One of the most unfortunate consequences of today's obsession with outdoor safety is that children are rarely left to play by themselves without a watchful adult. If a child is left unsupervised, it is seen as a sign of neglect. Increasingly, therefore, 'responsible parenting' is defined as protecting children from the experience of life.

In recent years, adult supervision has become both more expansive and more interventionist. Play has come to mean 'supervised activity'. Many parents have resolved their concern about the danger of the outdoors by opting for commercial, adventure play areas. Here, children can career around, climbing, sliding and swinging in perfect safety. Nets and barriers almost eliminate the risk of falls. Padding and mats prevent injury from knocks and tumbles. It seems like a great way to expose children to the thrills of scaling ladders and swinging on ropes, without the traditional accompaniments of splinters, rope burn and grazed knees.

But there is a downside. All of the activity is under the watchful eyes of parents and staff; all of it is shaped by what adults think children should do; all of it is ready and waiting. But as any child who has swung on a car tyre suspended over a stream knows, half the adventure is in building the swing – and most of the fun is in pulling your mates off it.

This restrictive approach towards play stifles children's initiative and desire for adventure. Supervised play is virtual play. Children need to play on their own – unsupervised activities are crucial for their development. For children to become responsible, they have to learn to make decisions for themselves, something they can never do under a parent's watchful eye.

Adult intervention also short-circuits the important process of children learning for themselves how to cope with challenging situations. Through unsupervised play, children can gain important insights about how to handle conflict, how far to go and where to draw lines.

There is no such thing as accident-free play. The attempt to abolish accidents from playgrounds means destroying the creative and challenging dimension of play altogether. Naturally, parents do not want to see their children get hurt. However, the occasional accident is a price well worth paying for allowing children the freedom to develop their initiative and skills. Serious accidents are rare and certainly far less common than in the past. Fortunately, when accidents happen, children show remarkable powers of resilience. Through such painful experiences, they learn about their strengths and weaknesses and, most importantly, assimilate important lessons about how to cope with adversity.

About the text

In 1994, the Hertfordshire County Council's Travelwise team in Great Britain organised the first walk to school week in the summer term with just a few of its schools. Since then, the campaign has become international and in 2001 two and a half million walkers took part.

Here is the leaflet that was produced to persuade parents and children to walk to school in 2001.

As you read, consider the following features of the text:

Word level

• The word choice indicates that this leaflet is aimed at adults. How might a children's version be different?

• Which adjectives and verbs give the leaflet a *positive* tone?

Sentence level

• The tense moves between the past, present and future to reflect the purpose of the leaflet.

Text level

• Layout and design is obviously very important.

• The text is divided into four sections with subheadings. What is the purpose of each of these sections?

• It includes practical information to enable you to join; why is this as important as the other information?

International
Walk to School Day

Tuesday, 2nd October, 2001

CALLING ALL SCHOOLS! Schools around the world will be joining forces again this year to celebrate International Walk To School Day on Tuesday October 2nd. This follows the outstanding success of last year's inaugural event, which saw some two and a half million children worldwide, accompanied by parents, teachers and community leaders, putting their best foot forward to promote the importance of walking to school.

Why Walk?

International Walk To School Day has proven to be an event which raises worldwide awareness of child pedestrian issues and provides a vast, accessible network for the exchange of experiences, ideas and information among schools in the participating countries.

It is much more than a one day media event. It has become a powerful partnership, building bridges across the health, education, environmental protection, safety and transportation sectors.

Experience has shown that walking to school together has a real purpose. It may be to increase physical fitness or to reduce traffic congestion; it can be a focus for learning vital road skills or creating a stronger sense of community; it could be used to promote safer routes to school and to reclaim the streets for pedestrians. Some walk simply because its fun, but everyone walks with one guiding principle: healthy people make healthy communities.

How to Get Involved

Check out the International Walk To School Day website at: www.iwalktoschool.org
There you'll find more details about the event, downloadable materials, innovative ideas and news from other countries, useful links and other resources.

 **iwalktoschool.org**

For those without Internet access, contact...
**Robert Smith, Road Safety Section, Environmental Services Directorate
Dorset County Council, County Hall, Dorchester, Dorset, DT1 1XJ**

About the text

In the 1950s *The Daily Mirror* newspaper (now *The Mirror*) led a campaign to abolish hanging. This editorial is a response to the execution of Ruth Ellis. She was the last woman hanged in Great Britain.

As you read, consider the following features of the text:

Word level

- What examples of very straightforward vocabulary can you find? Can you find any examples of slang?

- How many powerful verbs can you find?

Sentence level

- Look how many *if*s there are in the text. Why do you think this might be?

- Note the use of the future tense.

- The fifth paragraph is one long sentence. How effective is this? Find some other long sentences.

Text level

- The editorial is built around the idea of time passing, comparing what the reader might be doing (*fishing, lolling in the sunshine*) with what will be happening to Ruth Ellis. What is the effect of this technique?

- What examples of repetition used for effect, can you find?

- It addresses the reader directly.

- The ending breaks from this pattern by taking on the writer's opponents.

- The final image is poetic.

From The Daily Mirror, *13 July 1955. Ruth Ellis was the last woman to be hanged for murder in Great Britain.*

THE WOMAN WHO HANGS TODAY

*I*t's a fine day for haymaking. A fine day for fishing. A fine day for lolling in the sunshine. And if you feel that way – and I mourn to say that millions of you do – it's a fine day for a hanging.

If you read this before nine o'clock this morning, the last dreadful and obscene preparations for hanging Ruth Ellis will be moving up to their fierce and sickening climax. The public hangman and his assistant will have been slipped into the prison at about four o'clock yesterday afternoon.

There, from what is grotesquely called 'some vantage point' and unobserved by Ruth Ellis, they will have spied upon her when she was at exercise 'to form an impression of the physique of the prisoner'.

A bag of sand will have been filled to the same weight as the condemned woman and it will have been left hanging overnight to stretch the rope.

IF YOU READ THIS AT NINE O'CLOCK, then – short of a miracle – you and I and every man and woman in the land with head to think and heart to feel will, in full responsibility, blot this woman out.

The hands that place the white hood over her head will not be our hands. But the guilt – and guilt there is in all this abominable business – will belong to us as much as to the wretched executioner paid and trained to do the job in accordance with the savage public will.

IF YOU READ THIS AFTER NINE O'CLOCK, the murderess, Ruth Ellis, will have gone.

The one thing that brings stature and dignity to mankind and raises us above the beasts of the field will have been denied her – pity and the hope of ultimate redemption. The medical officer will go to the pit under the trap door to see that life is extinct. Then in the barbarous wickedness of this ceremony, rejected by nearly all civilised peoples, the body will be left to hang for one hour.

IF YOU READ THESE WORDS OF MINE AT MIDDAY the grave will have been dug while there are no prisoners around and the Chaplain will have read the burial service after he and all of us have come so freshly from disobeying the Sixth Commandment which says, 'Thou shalt not kill'.

The secrecy of it all shows that if compassion is not in us, then at least we still retain the dregs of shame. The medieval notice of execution will have been posted on the prison gates and the usual squalid handful of louts and **rubbernecks** who attend these legalised killings will have had their own private obscene delights.

Two Royal Commissions have protested against these horrible events. Every Home Secretary in recent years has testified to the agonies of his task, and the revulsion he has felt towards his duty. None has ever claimed that executions prevent murder.

Yet they go on and still Parliament has neither the resolve nor the conviction, nor the wit, nor the decency to put an end to these atrocious affairs.

When I write about capital punishment, as I have often done, I get some praise and usually more abuse. In this case I have been reviled as being a 'sucker for a pretty face'.

Well I am a sucker for a pretty face. And I am a sucker for all human faces because I hope I am a sucker for all humanity, good or bad. But I prefer the face not to be lolling because of a judicially broken neck.

Yes, it is a fine day.

Oscar Wilde, when he was in Reading Gaol, spoke with melancholy of 'that little tent of blue which prisoners call the sky'.

The tent of blue should be dark and sad at the things we have done this day.

rubbernecks people who stare foolishly